GARDENS IN THE MAKING

GARDENS · IN THE · MAKING

Gate. West Wittering.

By Walter H. Godfrey with illustrative Designs by the Author & Edmund L. Wratten.

CLASSIC EDITIONS

This edition digitally re-mastered and
published by JM Classic Editions © 2008
Original text © Walter H Godfrey 1914

ISBN 978-1-906600-04-4

All rights reserved. No part of this book subject
to copyright may be reproduced in any form or
by any means without prior permission in writing
from the publisher.

To
MRS. ILLINGWORTH ILLINGWORTH
this volume
is inscribed by
THE AUTHOR

PREFACE

SOME subjects are the copyright of a single pen, others invite the fancy and invention of many writers. The garden, even more than the house which it adorns, has in itself the seeds of such infinite variety that we would not lose a single volume from the growing library which is already dedicated to its beauty. Few writers can be without some useful thought to offer from their own experience, even if it be only to re-affirm an ancient principle, which, planted anew on some fresh page, may flower and bear fruit for many years to come.

This volume does not attempt to take the place of the architect or designer. It leaves, too, the choice of flowers and shrubs to the reader and his advisers, and deals entirely with the problems of lay-out, the general effect and the proper relationship of all parts of a garden to the whole. It desires to reach those who love their gardens and who like to think about them, and its aim is to stimulate thought and make clear the possibilities which lie as much in the smallest plot as in grounds of larger area.

There is a freemasonry among those who teach and those who learn in garden-craft, and their places are often and easily interchangeable. It is in this spirit that the following pages are offered to the reader.

WALTER H. GODFREY.

11 CARTERET STREET,
QUEEN ANNE'S GATE, S.W.,
April 1914.

PERSONAL NOTE

THIS little book is the outcome of much practical study of the principles of garden-design,—principles which are better understood, though not always more consistently followed at the present day, than when they were revived by the late George Devey and others in the middle of the last century. Penshurst Place was one of the first notable examples, foreshadowing the present "renaissance" of the formal garden, and Penshurst was the outcome of the united zeal of Devey and of his patron Lord de L'Isle. It has taken some fifty years for the leaven to work, and the change in public opinion has been aided by many enthusiastic writers and workers, but none were more steadfast in their support of the older and saner methods of planning than Mr. Devey and his surviving partner, Mr. James Williams. As pupils of Mr.

PERSONAL NOTE

Williams, and as his successors, the authors of the designs in the present volume have been trained in a tradition of formal gardening, not, indeed, in any extreme form, but after the manner of presentation in the following pages.

George Devey worked at a time when the battle of the styles was being fought and won,—when opportunities for improved "texture" in materials were not as plentiful as at the present day. His work, however (as shown, for instance, in the gardens of Coombe Warren), will bear the test of comparison with much good modern work, and his skill in enlarging a house to suit its surroundings is nowhere better shown than in the wonderful old-world gardens of Brickwall, Northiam.

The illustrations to the present volume, some of which were prepared with the help of Mr. James Williams, include a few adaptations from Mr. Devey's work and a number of original designs, a large proportion of which have been carried out. Grateful acknowledgment and thanks are due to the following for their kind permission to publish drawings of work executed or designed for them,—the Earl and Countess of Chichester, Stanmer, Sussex; the

Lady Margaret Duckworth and George H. Duckworth, Esq., Dalingridge Place, Sussex; Colonel the Honourable Herbert A. Lawrence and the Honourable Mrs. Lawrence, Ashdown Place, Sussex; the late Colonel C. J. Cotes, Pitchford Hall, Shropshire; Leopold de Rothschild, Esq., Ascott House, Bucks; Lawrence Currie, Esq., Coombe Warren, Surrey; Walter Monnington, Esq., Little Lodge, Newick, Sussex; Captain Price Wood, Henley Hall, Shropshire; J. C. Dun Waters, Esq., Plaish Hall, Shropshire; J. C. Hamilton Greig, Esq., Westerham, Kent; Arthur Edwards, Esq., Appledram, Sussex; and Mrs. Illingworth Illingworth, West Wittering, Sussex,—and to the Earl and Countess of Kenmare, for permission to include some portions of the beautiful gardens at Killarney which the late Countess of Kenmare designed and laid out herself, around the house which Mr. Devey built, and which was so unhappily destroyed by fire last year.

W. H. G.

In garden delights 'tis not easy to hold a mediocrity; that insinuating pleasure is seldom without some extremity.

SIR THOMAS BROWNE

CONTENTS

CHAPTER	PAGE
I. THE AIM OF THE GARDEN	1
II. FIRST PRINCIPLES	12
III. THE GARDEN PLAN	29
IV. FROM ENTRANCE TO COURTYARD	50
Entrance Gates and Lodges	50
The Approach to the House	57
Courtyards	60
V. GARDEN BOUNDARIES	71
Walls and Hedges	71
Gates and Gateways	86
VI. THE DIVISIONS OF THE GARDEN	94
Lawns and Bowling Alleys	94
Formal Flower Enclosures and Borders	99
Paving and its Uses	109
VII. THE TERRACED GARDEN	118
Terraces and Balustrades	118
Steps and Stairways	128

CONTENTS

CHAPTER		PAGE
VIII.	GARDEN FURNITURE AND BUILDINGS	139
	Seats and Arbours	139
	Loggias and Garden Houses	146
	Greenhouses and Orangeries	153
IX.	SOME OLD-WORLD FEATURES	156
	Arcaded Walks and Pergolas	156
	Topiary and the Labyrinth	161
	Treillage and Ironwork	167
X.	WATER, STONE, AND LEAD	172
	Pools and Fountains	172
	Figures and Vases of Stone and Lead	177
	Boxes and Tubs for Trees and Flowers	183
	Sundials	186
XI.	SOME SPECIAL GARDENS	190
	The Kitchen Garden	190
	The Town and Roof Garden	194
	Rock Gardens	200
PLANS	*Following page*	202
INDEX		205

GARDENS IN THE MAKING

I

THE AIM OF THE GARDEN

IT is not a rare occurrence to meet in the writings of gardeners, and of those who are skilled in the planting and nurture of flowers, a protest against the usurpation by the architect of any rights in the mystery and craft of garden-making. Horticulture is, indeed, a proud science, but its votaries surely assume too much when they state that a knowledge of plants and shrubs is synonymous with the power of design. On the contrary, it has been found that a striking gift in one department of garden activity is often accompanied by a total lack of perception in the other, and we shrewdly suspect that this notice of threatened prosecution to trespassing architects is issued by the authority of the head gardener,—not perhaps the least autocratic of men,—who fears some loss of prestige and some curtailment of his imperial and imperious sway.

The truth of the matter is that whereas gardening is a craft, and, if you will, a science, garden-design is an art, and requires different knowledge, and faculties of quite another order. The craftsman may sometimes be an artist, and the artist may occasionally include the craftsman, but their business is certainly not synonymous in detail or in kind. Their mingled duties are performed by thousands of people who desire nothing more than to have a garden of beauty, a place which will not only hoard each root and seed, but which will conspire to display the luxuriance of flower and foliage in all their surprising and reckless summer gaiety. Yet how far do they succeed? Up to a point, of course, they all succeed. A work that receives the ceaseless homage and industry of the crowd—such as is freely given to gardening and garden-making—cannot be wholly stationary or unsuccessful. And since the experience and invention of a number of minds have a cumulative effect, it is possible from the

Fig. 1.—Tennis Lawn, Killarney House, Killarney.

lower steps of the pyramid of general knowledge to rise with some care and thought to a more perfect attainment. But the passion for gardening among the majority of people unfortunately does not imply, at the present day, a widespread grasp of the principles of design. The untrained eye—and the age is full of untrained eyes where art is concerned—admires the effect of a skilfully planned garden, but is seldom capable of seeing that there are serious principles involved, or that without them such effects would be impossible. Moreover, it is infinitely easier to produce a fine bloom or a beautiful plant than to know where it should best be placed for its proper display. Popular knowledge is chiefly in matters of detail rather than of generalised principle, and gardening especially lends itself to the acquirement of multitudinous facts about individual flowers. This does not engender humility, and, as often as not, it breeds a prejudice against any serious arrangement, and chiefly against the formality of architectural planning. Yet this prejudice, like so many others, is more wilful than wise; it is the fruit of a gentle anarchic state of mind which fails to grasp the meaning of order and of design, and which fancies that it allies itself with Nature—that Nature which, nevertheless, responds so lovingly to the wise tuition of mankind. To those who still refuse to allow the architect a place in their garden councils, and who cling persistently either to the Victorian taste or to the purer joys of the wild garden and the "wilderness," we will submit only one plea. We beg them, as they have time and opportunity, to see the effect of rational planning in those fine old gardens, chiefly of the seventeenth century, that have reached such glorious maturity on the lines long ago laid down; and as lovers of architecture, and as lovers of flowers, we ask them to study the harmony, the fitness, and withal the rich luxuriance which these methods, properly carried out, display. It is not denied that the accidental effect of certain chance combinations of tree, shrub, flower and lawn may be very beautiful, nor can we even refuse our admiration to some wonderful specimen of a flower however ill-displayed; but a garden has a greater mission than to afford a merely fortuitous pleasure, its scope is far wider, and its contribution to the joy of mankind should be conceived on altogether a different scale. The garden should form almost as much the environment of our home life as the house itself, and while we love at times to be in touch with the unspoilt beauty of Nature, we shall still elect, as human beings, to employ the arts to surround us with the charms of order, arrangement, and carefully considered effect.

We shall take it as agreed then, between ourselves and our readers, that the architect whom we may have chosen to build us our house, to choose the aspect of our rooms, and to adorn the walls within which we are to dwell, shall not be prevented from completing his work in drawing out the main lines of the garden, nor be forbidden to harmonise the immediate surroundings of the building with the form of the fabric itself. The invention of the

FIG. 2.—Pitchford Hall, from the Stream.

architect—provided, of course, that we approve his taste—is as fittingly employed in those endless combinations of walls and hedges, of terraces and walks, of enclosed gardens and long borders of flowers, of lawns and pools, avenues and glades, as it is in the cunning manipulation of gables and chimneys, bay-windows and balconies, and all the other features that make up a beautiful architectural composition. Nor, in all this, need he attempt to interfere with the proper province of the gardener; he is the latter's ally, and prepares the way for him. For just as he foresees all the domestic wants in the planning of the house, and prepares it for the future work of the household, so he orders the garden for the gardener, and, having allotted the trees, the planting and the flowers their places, he can leave their care and often the choice of their species to those whose business and experience have fitted them for these duties.

We have said that the combinations of features which make up a garden are endless, and even that word gives but a poor idea of the infinity of varied effects which the skill of the artist and the activity of Nature can unite to produce. Exact repetition is almost impossible, for however closely one might seek to imitate an admired arrangement, a thousand chance happenings of weather, atmosphere, soil, surrounding features, and what not would give our imitation a character completely its own. We are wont to calculate an architectural effect with the most fastidious precision; yet often the result is not exactly what we intended. How much more, then, may it be said of garden planning, that we cannot anticipate in every detail the picture which our work will ultimately display—a picture, be it remembered, that will change with every hour, with every season, and with all succeeding years. Yet, if the simple principles have been rightly applied, we may be sure that the result will be fair to look upon, we may even be confident that we are building better than we know, and that the future will not fail to provide pleasure to all who walk in our garden, and will call forth words of appreciation concerning those who first traced the lines which Nature has since filled with her own lights and shadows and radiant colouring. Every artist knows that the medium in which he works must be studied and humoured before he can gain its

Fig. 3.—Design for Terrace at Ascott House.

secret; even the architect must woo the stone, the brick, the metal and the timber before he conquers their coyness and makes them respond to his will. Our mastery over the broad surfaces of the earth and over the living vegetation which it nourishes is even less complete, and nothing can be attained until we enter into a kind of partnership with them, since in return for our guidance they must needs do their part in fulfilling and amplifying our plans. The rules that we have made for other arts can scarcely be applied here, proportion and size refuse to be measured by any standard unit;—the house and the countryside make the conditions for our design, and as they vary in size and form, so our gardens must increase or diminish in length or breadth, must have important or unpretentious features, or must take their cue from the sum of their natural surroundings. Garden planning has therefore an elasticity in its scope, it presents a variety—even an uncertainty—which invites the fancy. It lends itself to broad and noble treatment, and also to an infinite ramification of detail; and it claims the aid of a hundred crafts to furnish and adorn it. But with all this it has greater need of

THE AIM OF THE GARDEN

direction, of obedience to a few guiding principles, than many a simpler and a more confined art. It is some suggestion of these principles which we wish to make in the following pages; they have their application to small and large gardens; they are the finger-posts to guide the direction of our invention.

II

FIRST PRINCIPLES

THE principles of garden design are more easily felt than formulated, and the subject scarcely admits of the strict definition or classification which we should apply to a science or a craft. We may observe, however, in the first place, that all arrangements, of whatever kind, should bear the impress of a direct and simple method. Second, that the aim should be to lay out and reveal the beauties of the garden by degrees, not with any forced intricacy, but by such means as shall give as much diversity and mystery as is consistent with simplicity of general treatment. Third, that each division of the garden should have its own special purpose, its own significance or meaning, and should be adorned with such architectural or other features as will sustain the interest and promote the usefulness of each part. By a careful observance of this rule we may avoid one of the severest criticisms of the careless plan :—that it is meaningless.

With these suggestions we may pair three other considerations of equal value. The simplicity of treatment should always be in the direction of utilising to their very best advantage whatever peculiar qualities the site may possess, or such as may be offered by the surrounding country. Second, the deft and skilful unfolding of the garden plan and scheme cannot be better achieved than by the use of well raised boundaries of stone and brick, yew, box or beech, such as will ensure the shelter and privacy of every part. For shelter and privacy are as essential to the grateful flourishing of all things planted in the garden as to the full use and enjoyment by its possessors ; and even where a distant view must be preserved, much can be done in framing and focusing its charm. And lastly, all the divisions and special features, in regard to their position and use, cannot be considered apart from the plan of the house itself, and many have placed as the very first requirement of design the strict unity of house and garden, in all its aspects.

Taking the twofold classification suggested above, our primary consideration in design should be *simplicity of treatment and harmony with existing conditions*. The stretches of lawn, the enclosures for pleasure gardens, the terraces, wide walks and greens should be rectilinear in outline as far as possible ; the paths should be straight, the planting should be formed in simple masses—the whole effect being well-balanced and restful. Isolated clumps of planting should be avoided, and single trees and shrubs where valuable enough to be preserved should be linked to boundaries or made to appear intentional objects in the general scheme. It often happens that such obstacles, unwelcome at first to the garden plan, provide it, in the end, with the happiest of its inspirations. It is much better to be directed by the conditions of the site, than to attempt to force some preconceived plan on a reluctant situation, and in drawing out the guiding lines it should be our object to find the simplest solution of the problems which the existing levels, aspect, trees, and other natural conditions present to us. Many are the failures in gardens which have resulted from violating this rule of simplicity of treatment and harmony

FIG. 4.—The Orangery, Coombe Warren.

with existing conditions. To many people simplicity spells poverty, and harmony is nothing so beautiful as contrast. Hence come those paths that are curved eternally until your eye longs for a straight line, feature crowded upon feature until each depreciates its fellow, and that planting which is of so foreign and imported a nature that it appears a stranger upon the hillside rather than a product of its own soil. But experience and good taste will dictate quite other methods. The garden should be a concentration of the beauty of the locality. Its native foliage, trees, even its own levels,—with proper correction,—should be retained as far as possible; other planting of a nature resembling that in the neighbourhood should be introduced to protect the walks and supplement the trees that are already grown; every view and distant prospect should be enhanced by the careful disposition of terrace and walk, of avenue and thick plantation. The garden should exhibit a superabundant wealth amid the richness of the countryside; it should shrink from many barren gravel paths, but should love a multitude of turf and paved walks; its trees should shun an unnatural isolation, but should glory in companionship; and its flowers, instead of being spread in scattered beds across the turf, should mingle their luxuriant growth in enclosures set apart for them, or fill wide borders beneath high walls and hedges and along the sunniest of the walks. Not only should natural foliage be preferred in general to that which is strange to the district, but it is well to extend the preference to the building material of which walls, terraces, steps, garden-houses—and even the house and outbuildings themselves—are made. Limestone, sandstone, chalk, flint, brick and tile, all have their peculiar suitability to their native places. So, by natural, restful, and simple means the garden shall arise from the countryside like a favoured child, more richly clad than its brother glades and meadows; and where the cultivated meets the wild land, some pleasant boundary can be set,—some quiet ditch of fern or sheltered path, or a " wild garden," can be planned between the woodland and the well-trimmed walks.

The second group of considerations counsels the designer *to avoid all inordinate display, and to cultivate privacy with that ample protection and shelter which makes for the maximum of usefulness and beauty in the*

18   GARDENS IN THE MAKING

Fig. 5.—Gateway and Yew.

garden domain. We may perhaps sum up the sentence in the single word "repose." The method of garden planning, as it is desired to present it here, is largely embraced in a process of dividing the garden into many gardens, each part having an organic relation with every other part, and all together forming one harmonised scheme. This principle is of the utmost importance. A formal garden enlarged to extravagant dimensions has a barren and hard effect which defeats its own object.

FIRST PRINCIPLES

On the other hand, an informal scheme is aimless and wearisome unless the site is particularly endowed by Nature, and is pleasantly broken up by majestic trees and other natural features. The majority of plants and flowers require a comparatively close range of vision for full appreciation, and blooms set in an enclosed garden or bordering a line of wall or hedge will have a far greater effect than if they are merely units in a wide and extended scheme. In most sites the question settles itself from the practical necessity of shelter, but the æsthetic point is of no less weight. It is rarely possible to compose a satisfactory picture, involving a large area to be seen in its entirety from the house, and in any case it will not have the same instant appeal that comes from the sectional garden with its luxurious features set in their proper background.

In advising the division of the garden, it is not suggested that the perspective of distance does not provide one of the most delightful pleasures to the eye, when it is skilfully preserved. But distance, unless it is the wide survey of many miles from a respectable height, requires the help of gradation. A long garden, giving on to a distant walk or avenue which leads the eye to some landmark or to the horizon, is a most dignified and always a pleasing device; and if its length is graduated by recurring trees and other features, it is much improved. Such a perspective is helped by a lofty wall, hedge, or bank of trees, which, being above the eye, carries an upper line to meet the converging boundaries of walk and border. It is the bird's-eye view which, though occasionally interesting, should be generally avoided, since one soon wearies of seeing too much, and of seeing it in an imperfect and indistinct manner.

The most important boundary to be introduced is that which separates the entrance from the rest of the site. In many modern houses there is no attempt to screen the private gardens from the road or drive, and the planting is often discontinued before the house is reached in order to expose and display the grounds. The result of this is a complete absence of shelter, the wind sweeps round the house, and every one who walks in the garden is visible, willingly or unwillingly, to the chance visitor. Occasionally the aspect of an existing building, or the difficult configuration of the ground, will make

FIRST PRINCIPLES

it impossible to shut off the entrance from the pleasure gardens; but the general rule, which can nearly always be followed with the exercise of a little ingenuity, should be a north entrance with the gardens south, east, and west. If the entrance can be made into a courtyard, with the help of outbuildings, flanking walls, etc., so much the better. A picturesque entrance is a great asset to a house, but its qualities should depend on graceful lines, good planning, and careful association with one or two well-grown trees, rather than on any attempt to combine it with the gardens themselves.

Along the principal garden-front of the house should extend the terrace or paved walk, which forms the highway between life within and without doors. Considerations of levels, existing trees, etc., will determine its width measured away from the house; but up to a certain point the greater the width the better the effect. If the gardens are on level ground and tend to be shut in, the space should be extended as far as is practicable in the form of a lawn; but if they slope away, the stretch of level terrace may be more contracted, though it is advisable to have a good width to ensure a restful stability to the appearance of the building.

This level platform is the key to the garden. It can be prolonged either way into a sheltered walk, covered or otherwise, which is thus easily accessible from the house. From it other walks and paths can be traced which shall divide the site into lawns, flower-gardens, terraces, and formal enclosures to a number equal to the fancy and resources of the owner. The ultimate design and situation of these apartments in the fairy palace of the garden will depend on a thousand considerations; but we must never forget that to ensure privacy and to provide a sustained interest, all the divisions must be self-contained, sheltered, and generally unapproached save by well-planned paths and archways—for the purpose of revealing their beauties one by one, and reserving the finest views and objects of most delightful interest to be enjoyed severally and at leisure. If the visitor sees everything as he arrives, he may indeed be struck by the great display, but his curiosity is not aroused nor is his imagination stimulated as in those gardens founded on earlier and surer principles, the attractions of which seem

FIG. 6.—Wrought-iron Gate beneath Trees.

to lure us to a continual round of discovery and at the same time to defy exhaustion.

In this connection it is necessary to point out the propriety of planning carefully the surroundings of foreign features if it is wished to introduce them. It is of undeniable interest to import various modes of garden-making from countries other than our own; but these methods should not be allowed to override the main scheme, which must be one which is suited to English soil and climate, and is in harmony with the best English tradition. A little care in choosing the site of such experiments and in making their situation one which will not compete with the rest of the garden, will prevent any serious incongruity from being felt.

Our third and last pair of considerations has to do with a *rational and purposeful plan of house and garden together*. There must be as much unity between each part of the house and the adjoining grounds as there should be between all parts of the garden. This right relationship will be strengthened if our planning is informed with some obvious reason for every detail of its arrangement, and the greater care we exercise the more likely is the plan to be permanent, adding beauty to beauty with every year until it acquires that "old-world" character which we all admire.

There are two ways of looking at the relationship of house and garden,—first, the garden as seen from the house; and, second, the house as approached from the garden. Both are of great importance from an æsthetic point of view, although the former has more claim to our practical consideration. The twofold problem presents itself in many different ways, being easier when we build a new house and plan its garden, than when we have to adapt both buildings and grounds already in existence and fairly matured. If we have a free hand from the start and our site is a new one, we can give due thought to our garden scheme in settling the disposition of the house, the position of its rooms, and the precise aspect of its windows. The general shape of the house, too, and its outbuildings can be arranged with a view to affording a background, the scale of which will suit the garden.

To take this second consideration first, we cannot be too often reminded how important a matter it is. Many good gardens are spoiled by the unharmonious or ineffective background which the house itself supplies, and some considerable architectural treatment of garden wall, arcade, or other buildings is necessary to restore the lost balance. The defect can be avoided by forethought where a new building is concerned, but when encountered in the case of existing buildings, it must be put right before anything else is done. For instance, we may find a beautiful lawn from which a fine prospect is obtained towards the south. Its boundaries west and east may be quite satisfactory, marked, let us suppose, by lofty trees. To the north, however, where the house lies, it has no regularity, the building is high with no length to form a fitting frame to the broad sweep of the turf; it is, moreover, placed awkwardly at one side, and the whole picture is marred. In this case it is necessary to make good with garden architecture the faulty background provided by the house. The straight walk between the building and the turf must be made the full length of the lawn. Pavilions or garden-houses might be built at each end, and these connected as far as the house by walls, pleasantly treated with brick and stone, or by an

FIRST PRINCIPLES

Fig. 7.—Elm Tree Farm, West Wittering.

arcade, a series of piers, or a pergola. By this means the house is made to spread itself along the ground, it is coaxed into performing its proper function in regard to the garden upon which it looks, and it is rid of the isolation which divides it from its surroundings. The whole appearance is transformed by the simple work of co-ordination. This problem of the house as viewed from the garden, and as an integral part of the design, must be considered in the same way that an artist considers the composition of a picture. What the abbey church is to the cloister, what the back scene is to the play, such is the relationship and harmony at which we must aim. Standing in different parts of the garden we must mark carefully the length, height, mass, and projection of the building, and determine what lines or features it is necessary to accentuate or to moderate. And when the house, with its adjoining buildings, terraces, and trees has provided us with a background which satisfies the eye, we can proceed with more certainty of success to the other problems of the garden scheme.

This is one aspect of the unity which is required between house and garden; the other, the garden as viewed from the house, we will now discuss in detail under various types of plan. What picture we shall prepare for each window and what devices we shall employ for pleasant and useful access from within to without doors, depend on the circumstances of each specific problem, and may be more clearly set forth by the examples which follow.

III

THE GARDEN PLAN

TO embark upon a successful argument our premises must be sound, and before we seek to lay out our garden we must make sure that our starting-point—the house—is rightly arranged for our enterprise. Let us therefore retrace our steps a moment. There are sites which present formidable difficulties of aspect, sloping away and hidden from the sun, with their views to the north, constraining us to do violence to all the normal canons of design. The greater number of sites will, however, allow us to place our building towards the south, or a few points east or west, to gain the full measure of sunlight which the climate will afford. As far as possible the southern, eastern, and western sides of our building should be devoted to the garden ; all the best rooms, both living and bedrooms, should look upon it; and the north should be reserved for the entrance, for corridors, passage-ways, and offices. If the house has wings, it is desirable that they should project north rather than south, for the entrance courtyard can thus be better defined and made more picturesque, while the garden front is left open to light and air. Projections, however, on the side of the pleasure gardens, if not too close together, can be made the occasion for many interesting arrangements.

A normal plan is seen in fig. 62, where the interrelationship of the house and its surroundings is clearly shown. The drive is brought along the northern side of the site to a courtyard, partly sheltered by the eastern or kitchen wing of the building. On the western side is a garage, which, while being in the most convenient position for the drive, extends the architectural background required for the garden. The grouping of the buildings as one approaches the entrance is of a picturesque informality, with just enough symmetry to give a dignified and orderly approach. The tall chestnut on the right furnishes the courtyard and overhangs the steep roof of the garage, which it unites with the

Fig. 8.—Plaish Hall, Shropshire.

house. The skyline and general grouping should have in themselves the elements of beauty, and an entrance should seldom require the help of flower-beds or borders. Its own lines and disposition should possess an attraction which is permanent and always suitable to its special function. The southern, western, and eastern sides of the house are thus left in complete possession of the gardens, which are effectively screened and sheltered from the drive. The principle is illustrated further in the plans of Stansted (fig. 59), Coombe Warren (fig. 60), and Henley Hall (fig. 61).

It often happens that an old house will have its principal entrance on the south side, and the gardens will be hopelessly cut up and exposed to view. This vital defect must always be remedied by diverting the approach, an operation that will not be found as difficult as it may appear. Pitchford Hall, near Shrewsbury (fig. 2), a beautiful half-timbered house of the sixteenth century, was sadly spoilt in this way. The main building, with two long wings stretching to the south, enclosed three sides of a quadrangle, and a fourth side had been added in the late eighteenth century. In the centre of this was the principal entrance, approached by a drive which crossed the rapid stream on the banks of which the house is built. The drive has since been diverted, and an entrance made on the north side; the later work is removed, and the quadrangle opened to the sun. By bringing the lawn within this, slightly terracing the banks of the stream, and arranging a path bordered by cut yews between the timbered wings, it has been possible to restore its gardens to the house, with all the serenity and beauty of turf, foliage, and water.

An equally striking example, but on a much smaller scale, is shown in the plan of Little Lodge, Newick (fig. 9). The original cottage was a parallelogram, having a living-room, kitchen, and two storerooms on the ground floor, and three bedrooms above. The entrance was in the flower garden, on the south side, opening into the living-room, while the kitchen garden was on the north, along one side of the drive leading from the road. As it was desired to add another sitting-room on the east side, it was necessary to cut off a portion of the two storerooms (now converted into one room) to form a passage, and here was the opportunity to make an entrance on

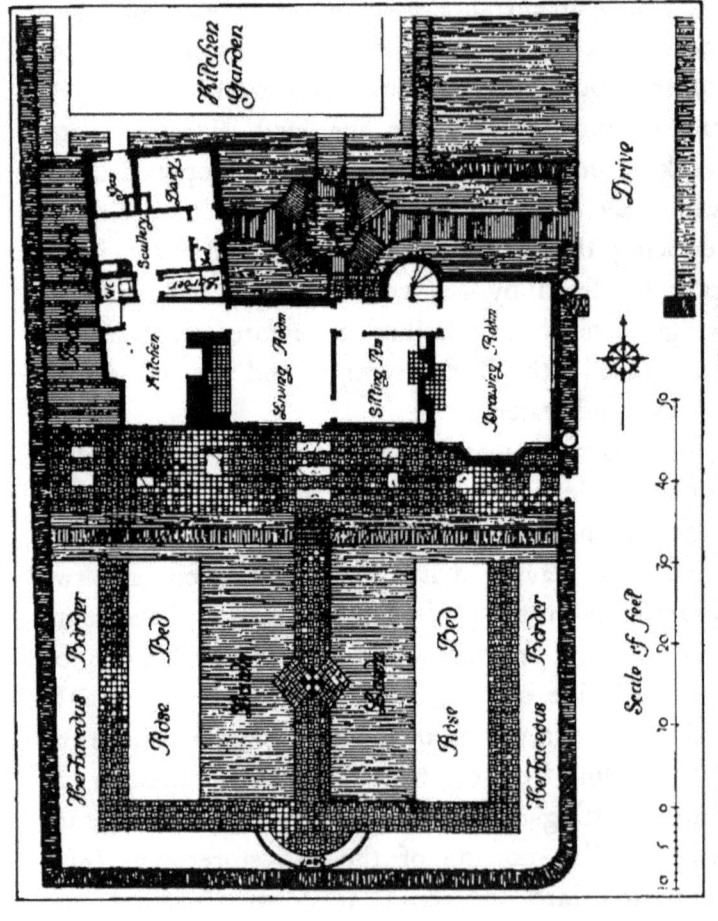

Fig. 9.—Little Lodge, Newick.

THE GARDEN PLAN

the north side. An extension of the kitchen provided the sheltering west wing, a little circular projecting staircase added to the picturesqueness of the entrance, and a cherry tree provided the centre for a paved court. The entrance was thus placed more conveniently for the drive, between the kitchen garden and the cottage, while privacy was restored to the flower garden on the south side.

The gardens at Elm Tree Farm, West Wittering (fig. 56), illustrate another method of surmounting a similar difficulty. Here the house faces south, and looks across a broad lawn to the road. The entrance was on the south front at its western end, and there was a drive which passed awkwardly from the road up the eastern side of the lawn, along the front of the house, and so to the stable-yard. It was not practicable to alter the position of the door without considerable expense; the drive, however, was removed and an ample carriage-way made direct from the road to the garage and stables. Carriages could thus set down within a few feet of the front door without intruding on the garden. The plan and view of Dalingridge Place, West Hoathly (figs. 10 and 57), show a circular entrance courtyard which occupies the western side of the house, leaving the south and east well screened from the drive and approach.

There are very few gardens in which this principle of privacy can be dispensed with, for there is nothing more troublesome than to be unable to enjoy security from interruption, or to be liable continually to be seen by all who call at the house. Even in small cottages the gardens of which lie between the front door and the road, it is generally possible to lead the path up one side of the plot and screen it from the private walks. This is not always necessary; the time-honoured straight path from the gate to the cottage porch, with the wide border of flowers on each side, should not lightly be displaced, for a hedge behind the border will protect a useful part of the garden and increase the effect. The cottager puts his whole display of flowers into the borders along his front path, and uses the remainder of the garden for vegetables. He gets in this way the maximum of effect with the minimum of expense. His plot is modelled on the kitchen-garden, and, like it, it cannot dispense with the middle walk edged with flowers; his garden is

THE GARDEN PLAN

usually too small to afford the division of area recommended for larger grounds.

We shall have a later opportunity for discussing the entrance courtyard in detail; our concern now is with the main lines of the plan. We will conclude that the entrance is set on the north side of the house, and that we now have to consider the main lines of the gardens proper.

The feature of first importance is the terrace or platform on which the house itself rests. The architectural character of a building practically demands that it should be raised from a level base, and that its immediate surroundings should have a formality which will harmonise with its own vertical and horizontal lines and set them off to advantage There is nothing that does this so perfectly as the paved terrace or walk carried along immediately adjacent to the principal garden front. The levels of the ground will determine whether the terrace will be raised from the surrounding garden, or whether it will be merely a paved walk at the same level. Equally suitable in tile or brick, York, Purbeck, or old London paving-stone, it affords an immediate dry walk when one steps out of doors; and besides providing the level platform that gives dignity to the house, it becomes, if continued to a proper length, the base line for the whole garden scheme. If the house is on a knoll or raised very much above the main garden, it may be necessary to remove the principal terrace some little distance away; but even then a short paved walk next the building will be necessary, with easy access from the one to the other. The same arrangement may become advisable where the house is sunk below its gardens—a situation which, though difficult, presents many attractive problems. Normally, however, the chief paved walk should be planned next to the building, with as many doors as convenient leading to it; and this should be the garden highway, every pains being taken to make it as attractive as possible.

Let us look at our plans again to see how the idea may be carried out. In fig. 62 we see the paved walk continued as a pergola both east and west. The centre portion gives the level open space so valuable for setting off the building; and its continuation each side being limited by the boundaries of the open site, is given interest and

Fig. 10.—Bird's-eye view, Dalingridge Place, West Hoathly.

distance by the colonnade of roses. The walk westward leads to the woodland and wild garden, and the whole extends the length of the house to correspond with the main width of the garden. Wherever one stands, therefore, in the walks below, one looks up to a background of which the house occupies the centre and the pergolas the two wings.

At Little Lodge, Newick (fig. 9), the ground was above the level of the floors, and the latter had to be lowered still further to increase the height of the rooms. The paved walk was therefore sunk below the level of the garden and made very wide to ensure the dryness of the house. It is of bricks laid in small squares, varied by flagstones, and is the full width of the enclosure.

At Elm Tree Farm, West Wittering (fig. 56), a broad walk of the beautiful Purbeck stone is laid along the front between the house and the lawn, and with its level character increases the quiet sobriety of the Georgian house. It is seldom, however, sufficient to take the paving to the end of the house, for all garden walks require distance and a continuation of their lines. At Elm Tree Farm, therefore, some outbuildings and planting were removed at the eastern end, the south wall of the house was continued in brickwork for some distance and with it the paved walk, which with the ascent of a few steps passed beneath some tall elms and terminated with a seat against a return wall. In this way a shady terrace was procured where shade was needed, a pleasant entrance to the flower garden was effected, and, most important of all, the walk by the house was given length and the charm of a graduated perspective.

The bird's-eye views of Dalingridge Place (fig. 10) and Plaish Hall (fig. 8) show further examples of the paved walk, the former being of London paving-stone, and projected to lead to steps and a seat beneath the fine trees at the west end of the terrace. A similar treatment is shown at Henley Hall (fig. 61).

Beyond the principal paved walk it is not easy to generalise on the further development of the plan, as the conditions attaching to various sites are so totally dissimilar. The division and subdivision of the garden will depend so much on natural boundaries, existing timber, and numberless accidents of view and aspect. Although by no means a rule to be always observed, it is yet desirable to have a stretch of lawn near the house, especially if there are good trees to back it up on one or both sides to group well with the house. The level, unbroken surface of the lawn and its quiet colour give the garden a sense of restfulness, and a sufficient area of turf is of the utmost value to the architectural character of the building. Care should be taken that this lawn is not needlessly broken up by beds of flowers, nor unduly intersected by paths. The continuity of the green surface is its chief quality, and small patches of grass are seldom effective. It is a different matter, of course, with grass paths, which, either as long narrow walks, or paths of equal width forming the pattern of a flower garden, are in themselves very beautiful. Such paths can be easily mown on account of their uniformity, and the broad surface of a lawn presents no difficulty to the machine; but when it is cut up with "bedding out" it is a costly and trying process to keep trim, and the results are out of all proportion to the labour involved.

A lawn, if of sufficient extent, is greatly enhanced by rectilinear boundaries, but on one side at least it may lose itself under the shade of tall trees. If the limiting hedges and walls are too low, the

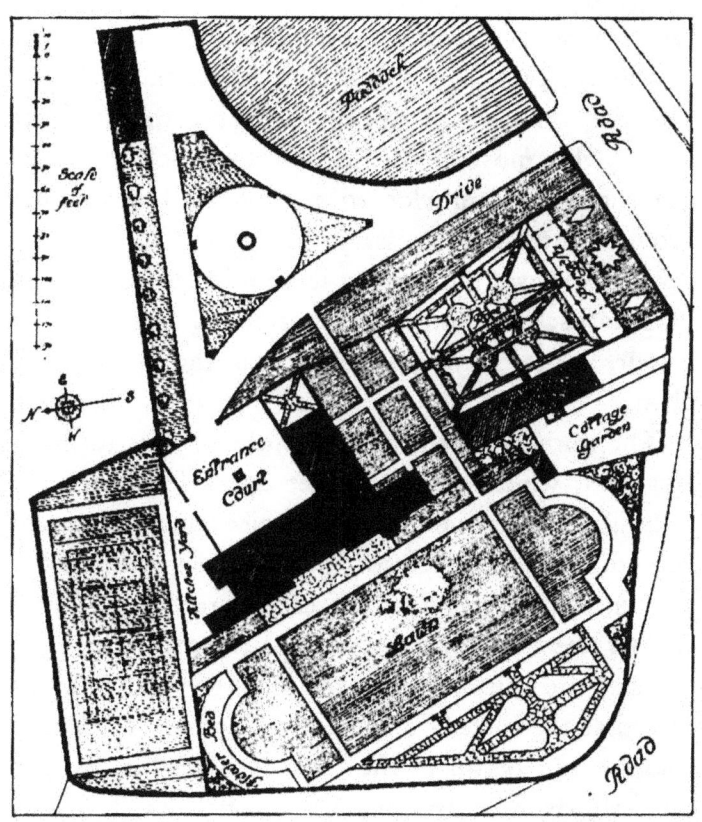

Fig. 11.—Tower House, Appledram.

appearance may be flat and uninteresting ; but the background of a long building, a high bank of trees or a lofty yew hedge, will give it depth and richness, and the shadows of foliage cast on the turf are among the most beautiful effects which a garden can show. A well-clothed pergola will sometimes provide just the necessary strength of outline to give to a lawn the beauty it should possess, and a long herbaceous border, fully stocked with glowing colour, is perfect when seen across the level green plain.

The number of enclosures, more or less formally arranged, which are to be set apart for flowers is unlimited, and one or two choice flower gardens should be planned close to the house, with special reference to the windows of certain rooms. Where the terrace and lawn lie along the principal front towards the south, formal gardens can generally be placed at the eastern and western ends. They may also be set between the terrace and the turf, if properly defined, and in this position their beauty will be increased if they are slightly sunk in the ground.

At West Wittering a formal garden is shown to

the west, just beneath the window of the principal sitting-room (figs. 28 and 56). The same position is similarly occupied at Ascott House (fig. 30), Henley Hall, Ludlow (fig 61.), and Coombe Warren, Kingston Hill (fig. 60). A position has been left for a formal garden to be seen from the drawing-room windows at the east end of Dalingridge Place (fig. 57), and another adjoins the lawn at Plaish Hall (fig. 8). In the plan on fig. 62 a rose garden is shown to the west between the garage and pergola, and two others below the pergolas on each side of the lawn.

These little gardens, set in carefully chosen places, do not derange the general lay-out; they concentrate the gaiety and brightness of colour and form, and the eye is led along the broad borders to expect their repetition at no great distance. Lower levels overlooked by terraces are readily treated in this way and present a feast of colour, inviting us to descend among them.

Where the whole area is small and there is not room for much turf, or where the only lawn is to be occupied by a tennis court and the rest of the ground to be devoted to flowers, it is advisable to

Fig. 12.—Formal Garden, Henley Hall.

treat the entire site as a formal flower garden. Care, however, should be taken to keep the outlines simple and to avoid the imitation of too architectural or grandiose a design in so limited a space. A certain amount of formal planning is essential to give the flowers their full effect, and some fanciful forms of cut yew, box, etc., are not out of place in a cottage garden; but formal design can be easily overdone, and will thus defeat its own object. It is an art which should conceal its art, guiding the effect without obtrusiveness, introducing a quiet orderliness without advertising its purpose too loudly. Only in the town garden should the architectural lines be strongly predominant, for reasons which will be discussed more fully on a later page.

One word more with regard to the general plan. It must never be forgotten in our extensions of the garden scheme that it is as necessary to co-ordinate every part as it is to harmonise the house with its surroundings. The idea of "composition" must never be absent from our minds, and the connecting links :—paths, walks, terraces, steps, arches, etc., must be carefully thought out. It will be an advantage if we can extend the garden gradually year by year, for we shall then accustom ourselves to each addition as it is made, and familiarise our eyes with the way in which the whole composition is being formed. For example, it will often be necessary on a sloping site to correct the awkward lines of certain levels by throwing out "bastions," or by excavating to reduce the height of the ground. The levels above the rose garden at Ashdown Place, Forest Row (fig. 58), presented a formidable problem before they were reduced to terraces ; and even then the general slope of the surroundings rendered the result unsatisfactory until the middle or cross terrace was extended, on one hand into the side of the hill, and on the other to form a raised platform towards the falling country. This cross terrace, or bowling-green, is long enough to "steady" the whole composition, and affords, moreover, a fine point of vantage from which to command the view. The very wide flights of steps (fig. 35) were specially designed to prevent the imprisoned appearance which would otherwise have been given to the rose garden, and the blocks of cut yew at either end were devised to screen the diagonal fall in the ground, and to give the appearance of stability to the steps. A somewhat similar terrace with bastion-shaped end is to be seen at Dalingridge Place (fig. 10), where the direction of the falling ground is also diagonal to the plan of the house. These are but instances here and there of a thousand problems which, if not squarely met and solved, are sufficient to cripple the best schemes and leave a lasting sense of dissatisfaction.

Having dealt broadly with the principles of design, and with those considerations which should determine the general plan, we are now free to examine the details in their proper sequence. It is an easier task, for it brings our subject within the readier compass of our vision. Moreover, to examine the garden *seriatim* is a more natural process than to attempt to take its full compass in one view. The art that should be concealed must suffer from exposure even in a treatise,—howsoever worthy the intention,—but every one may appreciate such recommendations as apply to single features or well-defined situations. Those, therefore, who neglect our earlier pages may yet linger not unprofitably for a few hints on points of detail.

IV

FROM ENTRANCE TO COURTYARD

Entrance Gates and Lodges

IN choosing the entrance to our grounds, let us seek the place where the trees are of the finest growth,—where some giant oak or sycamore, or better still some evergreen, ilex, or holly provides a fitting arch of shadow and wall of green. Trees to an entrance are like supporters to a coat of arms; they give dignity even to a cottage gateway. Wherever possible, let the entrance be recessed, so that the flanking wall or hedge may leave a margin of well-mown turf against the roadside. The entrance is the outward sign and indication of the house within—to the passer-by it represents the whole estate, to the visitor it is the prologue of the play. It should therefore be well considered, and money spent upon it will always more than repay the outlay.

The simple gateway will be discussed on a later page, but there is certainly nothing more excellent than a good wrought-iron gate and properly proportioned piers of brick or stone. The illustration in fig. 22, a design adapted from an old example at Croydon, and the arched gateway at West Wittering which forms the title-page to this volume, show two methods of treatment. It depends entirely upon the design and the method of its execution whether such an entrance shall have an inviting or forbidding aspect. Between the present day and the more spacious times of the eighteenth century, when the wrought-iron entrance gate was brought to its perfection, we have had a long period of shameful degradation. The gates and railings of cast-iron, produced by the thousand to commercial patterns, have been used *ad nauseam* in town and country alike, and the dislike which they have called forth is often too strong to be discriminating. But let a simple design be prepared and the work entrusted to an intelligent village smith, and we may rest assured that the forged bars and scroll work will be as attractive as the miserable cast ornament had been repulsive. It is not that cast-iron is unsusceptible of charming treatment in the right place, but there are many reasons for excluding it from garden architecture. On the other hand, wrought-iron is a ready ally in our garden schemes; it is increased in beauty when near to masses of foliage or flowers, and its fanciful lines of sombre colour allow us to see beyond them and even invite our view.

The character of the grounds into which the entrance leads will have largely to determine for us our treatment of the entrance itself. If we have perforce to go straight into a garden from the road, it becomes merely a question of choice between the many types of gates and archways which we shall discuss later. The chief consideration in such cases is generally to prevent too much publicity, and the arched opening in a high wall or hedge will appear almost the sole alternative to a solid doorway. In the latter case there are many quite simple and attractive methods by which the entrance can be marked and an architectural compensation provided for the loss of prospect within. The solid door

FIG. 13.—Lodge and Gates, The Mount, Westerham.

should be of oak framing, moulded to suit the style employed, and in any case should have an appearance of strength and durability.

More usually however, if there is space to follow the general principles already set forth, we shall enter upon a forecourt, or a drive leading thereto, and we shall not be hampered by questions of privacy or exclusion. Indeed, the entrance is such a point of vantage to survey the courtyard itself, or the sweep of the drive through the grounds, that we can afford to be generous to the passer-by and give him as good a view as our opportunities will allow. The aim should be, whether by simple or more elaborate means, to invest the threshold of our estate with a suitable dignity, the design of which may still be picturesque and imaginative in quality. The day has happily gone by when "rustic" lodges were fashionable at the park gates, and a perverted sentiment refused a legitimate architectural treatment where it was obviously demanded. From the beginnings of its history, architectural art has never been more fittingly applied than when used in the shaping and embellishing of entrance gates and archways, and although it will suit neither the purse nor the taste of every one to produce an elaborate design, it is certain that the entrance loses immensely in character if the architectural idea is eliminated. If the gates are linked with a gatekeeper's lodge or other buildings, every opportunity is afforded for pleasant grouping and a good effect. A simple example of a lodge and oak gates is that at Westerham (fig. 13), but here the lodge has been treated as an isolated cottage. Wherever the building can be definitely joined to a brick or stone archway or to piers, a variety of delightful architectural studies are possible in every phase of the Renaissance from Jacobean to Georgian. To gain symmetry the lodge can be repeated on the opposite side—thus providing a second cottage, which is often required; and if the whole group is built of a roughly worked stone or hand-made brick, an effective composition is made easy. Above all things it is important to avoid anything tame and commonplace, without character or diversity of outline. Mere originality and frivolous detail should, of course, be shunned, for they also defeat the essential qualities which are needful in the entrance. Sturdiness and dignity, a composition purposeful

56   GARDENS IN THE MAKING

Fig. 14.—Brick Gateway.

yet restrained, a striking skyline in the grouping of lodge and gates,—these, combined with scholarly detail and good workmanship, are required for complete success. A great deal can be effected by the plan alone of the space before the entrance, and a skilful arrangement will invest a simple oak fence with interest. As a general rule, a strict formality is a virtue, and as far as possible the domestic character of the lodge should be concealed or merged into the expression of its more important function as a sentry by the gate. The whole entrance, even in its most modest phase, is in the position of a frontispiece, and it should be worthy of its public position and the place of honour which it is its duty to fill.

The Approach to the House

The drive from the lodge gates, if of any length, is little different from a beautiful country road save in its privacy. Its course will be determined by the contour of the ground, and it will have to be formed in a substantial manner to stand the wear of heavy traffic. Through an undulating park it can follow the devious curves which the way of least resistance offers, and it is permissible to fetch a wide circuit to reach a fine view or pass through a beautiful glade. The formality of the garden does not require its extension into the surrounding estate, which is nothing more than an enclosed portion of the countryside, and it is a laudable desire to make the drive through the property as beautiful and varied as possible. In a flat country there is more need of artificial aids to obtain a good effect, and this may be done in various ways.

A long avenue of lofty trees is the noblest approach that a house can possess, but those who have the courage to plant them will do so with the knowledge that they will scarcely enjoy the fruits of their labour. Fortunately we still have amongst us men who sow for a future generation to reap, and indeed it is only right when we think of all that we inherit from the past. A fine avenue of trees is a priceless gift to the future, and its long and lofty bank of foliage is almost as beautiful, when viewed from the outside, as from within the perspective of its narrowing walls of green.

Where a house stands not far from the main road a straight avenue is of great value. It adds to its dignity, it makes the distance appear longer, and while exposing the centre of the house it screens the greater part of the building from the gate. Even an avenue of comparatively low pollarded trees acts as a charm, and a double line of fruit trees forms a fitting approach to a farm-house. The thorn is also an excellent tree for an unconventional avenue. Its well-shaped heads of foliage are balanced on stems of variable shape, and from each season of the year it claims a special glory.

As we approach the house from the longer drives it will be well to introduce the formal character by degrees. The last part of the road should be straight, and preferably should lead direct to the entrance courtyard with this side of the house in full view, closing the vista. It is sometimes necessary to pass into the forecourt in a direction parallel with the house, and here great care must be taken to screen the drive from the pleasure gardens and the windows that overlook them. If possible, however, the drive should turn direct to the house, and the eye be led by avenue, hedge, or wall to the building towards which the road is leading. The surprise at suddenly turning a corner and finding ourselves by the front door is not to be compared in point of pleasure with the gradual approach in a straight line.

As the drive nears its destination, it may first be partly enclosed by planting, with banks of rhododendrons or other flowering shrubs, forming a foreground in the final stretch of straight road. Beyond, the lines can be taken up by sentinel Irish yews spaced widely apart in a deep grass border on either side. Further still some cut squares of yew, holly, or box, some stone piers and perhaps an archway of stone or brick will mark an added architectural character up to the point at which will rise the roofs of the house itself. All the materials are here for a fine picture, which can be varied indefinitely in its composition—an open country lending itself to large effects and enclosed areas or heavily timbered estates to well-defined and sheltered roadways. When all is said a line of trees remains the ideal condition for the approach to the house; bordering the simplest roadway they bestow upon it a quality and distinction obtainable in no other way, and even in winter such trees as stand by the carriage-way to Little Lodge, Newick (fig. 16), invest the cottage with much of their own beauty.

Courtyards

An enclosed space may by its fashioning be the pleasantest place on earth; it may also be the dreariest. The courtyard of the manor-house, the college quadrangle, or the cathedral cloister, the Italian *cortile* and the Spanish *pateo*,—all these are examples of the restful beauty which can be had by a little skilful handling. Given the eye of an artist, there are very few buildings which do not suggest by their own arrangement or that of their surrounding walls and boundaries some easy conversion into this, the simplest and most beautiful contrivance of architectural planning. The essence of design is to let the structure of the house or the conditions of its site suggest an idea, and then to use our invention and ingenuity in working it out to its own charming conclusion, and if on no other side of the building, that facing the entrance is almost certain to lend itself to the courtyard treatment.

It will be remembered that in our ideal house plan we have assigned the entrance to the north, leaving the south, east, and west to look out upon the pleasure gardens and private walks. The windows of the principal living-rooms and bedrooms will therefore be on the garden sides, and the entrance outlook will be confined as far as possible to the hall, corridors, offices, etc. If this arrangement has been followed it is obvious that the forecourt and the side of the house immediately facing it will require a treatment in which dignity, restraint, or a

Fig. 15.—Stone Gateway.

formal precision is the chief quality. Without perhaps going so far as to say that there is any position in which flowers are out of place, it may yet be conceded that the entrance court is not in need of beds of flowers for its adornment. Indeed, it is most successfully treated without their aid, and the combination of wall, hedge, gravelled court, and broad border of turf will be found to provide the best material for its composition.

Although, in our aim at restraint and a simple dignity, we may make a rule to dispense with flowers, it does not follow that the forecourt should be necessarily formal or rigidly symmetrical. A perfectly balanced architectural treatment can, of course, be made very beautiful, and represents perhaps the ideal method to be employed. But some houses will not stand too much severity, and where the building itself is not symmetrically designed,—a succession, maybe, of ivy-clad gables of no particular size or grouping,—there are many ways of ensuring dignity and restraint without recourse to an unbending formalism. And even in the most carefully prepared design, a fine tree, or group of trees, can never be considered as an intruder. Trees that are beautiful and well-proportioned in themselves can stand almost anywhere in the garden design, and will invariably increase the effect. Certainly they nowhere help the grouping so much as when they stand comparatively near the building and throw their shade across the forecourt, and the position of a good tree is often sufficient reason to plan the entrance courtyard so that its stem may be included within the boundaries.

It must be our aim, then, to blend the house, forecourt, and the surrounding trees into one satisfying picture, restrained in colour, but striking and impressive in form. And how many compositions are there which this enticing subject will suggest! Here, we may see a timbered house of low proportions, with steep pitched roofs of tile and soaring chimney-stacks, combined with close-cut hedges of yew, which themselves provide a deep green entrance arch or sturdy piers with curiously clipped finials. There, a stone manor-house worthy of Inigo Jones, its orderly ranks of windows ranged on either side of the doorway, and its hipped roof set above a bold cornice, with its forecourt enclosed by high stone walls, well coped and chased with

Fig. 16.—Little Lodge, Newick. The Approach.

niched recesses, and entered by tall twin pedestals crowned with vases of lead or stone. Again, a mansion of Tudor outline—a crowd of brick gables, oriels, lofty chimney shafts, and turrets—will wait to receive us behind its gatehouse, where its turf-bordered court is bounded by high trees or set within a frame of low walls studded with pyramids of yew. Or, the ample comfort of a house such as Wren loved to build will furnish its forecourt with fine wrought-iron work in a long screen with central gates, and perhaps on either side a colonnade with low pavilions. And so in endless variety we can trace the underlying idea of an orderly and conventionalised area set about the entrance door of the house, partaking of its architectural character, but at the same time proving itself an integral part of the garden scheme.

It is important that the entrance courtyard should require as little labour as possible in its upkeep, so that its appearance shall not suffer from any chance neglect. In these days of motor traffic it will have to be wide, and a circle of some 70 to 100 feet in diameter is not too much to allow, if vehicles have to pass in and return by the same road. It can be relieved by a centre-piece for which it should not be difficult to choose an effective feature. A square of turf or stone paving, with a clipped tree set in the ground or in a tub, a fountain with moulded parapet, a figure of stone or lead or a maze of dwarf box hedges will adorn the central space, and will prove valuable in adding definition to the quadrangular or circular treatment. It is often necessary to sink the courtyard to a level lower than the surrounding ground, and the necessary retaining wall will provide excellent material for a formal treatment of the boundaries. It is as well, in such cases, to avoid grass banks or so-called "rockeries"; the grass slope is better confined to the gardens themselves, and rock plants should have a domain of their own with a background of green to show up their masses of brilliant colour.

Courts other than those to the entrance provide endless scope for an inventive fancy. Whether enclosed on three sides or wholly within the buildings it should be possible to make them gay with flowers, with some special setting or background to complete a choice and alluring picture. Unless they are very large, it is difficult

FIG. 17.—Bird's-eye view of House with two Courtyards.

to bring enough sunlight into such enclosures, and it is therefore all the more important to repair the loss by an excess of colour. When completely enclosed the whole area should be paved, raised beds, tubs, vases, etc., being arranged for the reception of flowers, which can be introduced in full bloom and be replaced as soon as the blossom is over. Dwarf trees in boxes and a variety of stone and lead ornaments are to be found, suitable for mingling with the flowers, although care is required in their choice and arrangement. Water can be introduced in the midst, or a good central feature may be formed by a moulded stone curb as for a fountain,—circular, octagonal, or foliated in plan,—but filled with a mass of flowers instead of water from the midst of which a slender figure or finial can emerge. Balconies above with boxes of flowers and hanging blooms will give an added beauty and will lighten the whole effect.

Larger quadrangles will admit of arcaded or colonnaded cloister walks, wichuriana roses can be trained up the pillars, and turf can be used in the formal design of the ground. Here, however, the whole resources of the formal garden are open to us, and these will be considered on a later page.

One point is worth mentioning in connection with courts enclosed by buildings on three sides only. It is often difficult to make any self-contained arrangement which does not look mean and insignificant. The fact that one side is open makes it impossible to set one's own scale, for the country beyond will immediately challenge it. But a solution may sometimes be found in projecting the width of the court some distance out into the gardens by extending its parallel boundaries with dwarf hedges, walls, ·or balustrade, furnishing it the while with some feature of interest,—a seat, arbour, steps, or other device. By this means our court partakes of the garden,—a definite portion of the latter is received into the court, and that which cannot be treated satisfactorily by itself is blended with a larger scheme and its deficiencies are cancelled. The bird's-eye view of Dalingridge (fig. 10) will give an instance of the idea in practice.

V

GARDEN BOUNDARIES

Walls and Hedges

THE main business of garden design has already been defined as a skilful division into many gardens. Just as a house requires several apartments, and as its usefulness depends on a careful disposition of its rooms and corridors, so a garden demands separation into its manifold parts. It is in the art of this division and subdivision that we must bring the whole store of our knowledge and all the resourcefulness of our invention, for an initial mistake may mar our later schemes, and to alter it later will set back the garden development and bring disappointment in its train. There is plenty of scope for wide differences of taste in this matter, but even those who desire the broadest garden landscape must sketch in the structural lines of their picture with dividing walls or hedges. Such grandiose schemes are, however, for the few, and in the majority of both large and small gardens it will be found that the division into self-contained and sheltered areas provides the greatest charm, variety, and interest, besides allowing the opportunity for an unlimited variation in the style of gardening and in the natural and artificial features employed. The chief need of the garden—shelter, and its most elusive charm—mystery, alike demand the dividing lines of wall or hedge to separate its lawns and walks, and its many sites for the concourse of leaf and flower.

The most important matter in building a garden wall is to steer safely between two equally undesirable extremes. The material used must not be of so unyielding a nature that it repels the impress of time and weather, nor should it, on the other hand, partake of that tasteless and formless character known to misguided enthusiasts as "rustic" work. The one is as fatal as the other. A wall is a piece of building, it is architectural in its nature, and should have that quality of precision in form and outline which architecture demands. Yet it must be of the garden, it must not intrude, and it must

Fig. 18.—Design for Terrace, Ascott House.

readily yield to the natural processes which will mellow and soften its surface. No amount of architectural form or ornament need necessarily be out of place, always provided it is well designed and in a material which harmonises with the vegetation around it. In an old garden it is often the most startling architectural conceit of the early builder which pleases us most ; but this is because his stone and his brick have long since lost every trace of artificiality, until they have seemed a natural growth, so transformed are they by their dress of creeper, moss or lichen, or by the buffetings of a century or two of storms. A good deal is heard at the present time of " texture " in building materials, and since it often represents a fad or the desire for a false appearance of antiquity, we are apt to give the expression a wide berth. It remains, however, precisely the word to employ in the matter of garden walls and buildings, for the surface should have a texture sufficiently rough to invite the action of the weather upon it, to aid the growth of creepers and parasitic plants, and to blend its colour and tone with the living vegetation in the midst of which it is placed. Many otherwise admirable gardens of the past century seem to lack all the poetry and charm which we instinctively desire, for the simple reason that the stone and brickwork are of so finished and hard a character that Nature expends herself in vain upon their unresponsive surfaces. The immaculate stone steps and terra-cotta vases, smooth red-brick walls and heavy York-stone copings—these are enemies in possession, there to subdue the light-hearted gaiety of nature, instead of enjoying the gentle conquest which might beautify and enrich them in the end. This extreme artificiality had its natural reaction in the "rustic" walls and "rockeries" with which the past generation endeavoured to propitiate the sylvan deities. Such attempts overdid their intention, they out-Heroded Herod, and by their coarseness prevented all the delicate colouring and slow softening of outline—the *nuances* and half-shades which Nature loves unaided to express. These "rustic" extravagances point one moral—that the design of a garden should be in the hands of a trained artist, or should never be attempted until its principles have been studied with care, and its elements thoroughly mastered.

Fig. 19.—Oak Gate.

Wherever there is local stone no trouble should be experienced in raising gardens walls. Ashlar (that is, smooth worked stone in regular courses) should be employed only where important architectural work is to be carried out, although softer stones such as Ham Hill may be used more freely in this form, as their surface takes on a beautiful colour in weathering. Ragstone or even chalk can be built up in roughly squared blocks with irregular face, but the most pleasing method for ordinary walling will be found in using laminated stone in rough courses of two to three inches in depth. The stone walls of the Cotswolds, often built dry or with only a little mortar in the centre of the wall, are among the most beautiful kinds to be found. The long lines of irregular deep joints separated from one another by comparatively thin layers of stone, seem to give the wall a fine continuity, and the joints hold the shadow and diversify the surface. A good many local varieties of stone can be treated in this way, and as long as they are provided here and there with piers, gateways, or other features to furnish relief, these types of dry walling will always prove the most fitting for ordinary work.

Purbeck, York, and other stones used for paving lend themselves admirably to this method. In laying the stones, the courses may be irregular and varying in thickness, but the bed of the stones should be level; random work with varying angles is too disquieting to be satisfactory, and it will be found well worth the trouble roughly to square all large stones before setting them in the wall. At all costs avoid the artificially rough face with tooled edges which, fitting though it may be in the rusticated masonry of a large building, is quite out of place in its modern degraded form in a garden wall.

When the wall is to be of brick, care should be exercised in the choice of colour. The bright tints of the flowers and the fresh green of the opening yew will quarrel with the majority of ordinary red facing bricks. It is much safer to use a dark or brindled stock, for it acquires a neutral tint that harmonises with the natural colouring. Dutch bricks form a pleasant variation and are good in scale and colour, while many successful combinations of brick and stone or brick and tile may be made, according to locality and circumstances. If old

WALLS AND HEDGES

materials can be obtained, it is a great gain; for Time is the garden's ally, and whatever has his seal upon it has already a free passport into its friendly community.

There are many ways of adorning a garden wall, from the simple and utilitarian features of piers and buttresses to the purely decorative devices of moulded panels and string courses, of shaped openings or terra-cotta medallions. There is no space to stay over these details here, but there is one feature in common to all walls which we cannot pass over, for it combines a strict utility with a very strong influence upon the general appearance. We refer to the coping. Every wall should have a proper coping set in cement, to prevent the penetration of rain to the masonry or brickwork below. Numerous varieties can be seen in different parts of the country, and few are without a certain charm of their own. The simplest form is a double course of roofing tiles (called tile-creasing) projecting an inch or two to throw off the water, and a row of brick "headers" above them to keep them in place. This is quite as suitable for a stone as for a brick wall, and gives precision to the skyline. Care should

Fig. 20.—Wrought-iron Hand-gate.

be taken to lay the tiles (which are cambered) with their edges sloping downwards; and where tiles with "nibs" are used these may be left on the lower course to add to the interest. A double course of stout slates can be used in place of tiles, and the coping-bricks can be rounded or chamfered instead of being square. A moulded stone coping or one of flat York stone is quite serviceable; but it is important when the stone projects to see that its depth is not great, otherwise it will appear heavy. Refinement in the projecting lines of a coping is as important as refinement in the eaves of a building, and although a cornice may be in certain positions of considerable size it should be divided into several members of which the one with the greatest projection should be thin and clear-cut against the sky. Thus, there are many copings which are built up like miniature roofs over walls, some thatched, some tiled, and others of chamfered brick or stone. In each case the same rule holds good, the part defining the projection requiring a clear thin line. A very thick wall will, of course, take a heavier coping than a thin one, but more judgment is required in adapting the size to the varying heights than to the thickness. It will often be found that a lofty wall will look best with a comparatively slight coping, for the greater expanse of its surface gives it a slighter appearance. On the other hand, a low wall, the thickness of which is readily seen, will stand a heavy coping with several oversailing courses of brick. An open balustrade of shaped tiles, brick, or stone balusters is especially applicable to the latter, and will be noticed in detail later on. Hand-made ridge-tiles, whether circular or angular, combined with tile-creasing make an excellent coping, and they easily adapt themselves to positions where the wall changes in height, placed either in crow-stepped fashion or sloping down in a long straight ramp.

In laying out the direction of our stone and brick walls, we should never be forgetful of the possibilities of variations in plan. Instead of stretching the wall in a straight line from point to point, we can here and there recess it in square or circular bays; we can take it round an angle in a segmental or elliptical sweep, or we can break it backwards or forwards to give definition to a change in the garden treatment, or to afford greater prominence or beauty to a tree or shrub. Moreover, we can change its level for a similar purpose, and decrease its height at given points for the advantage of the view or to discover some fine mass of foliage.

More particularly do these considerations of plan and elevation apply to cut hedges of yew, box, beech, and the like; for, pre-eminent as these hedges are as division boundaries for the garden, they are not susceptible of the same architectural treatment as a wall of brick or stone. Nothing gives greater dignity, even majesty, to the garden than the giant hedges of clipped yew that we have inherited from the past. And for the reason just given we shall find that these hedges have been planted in a hundred different ways to obtain every advantage in plan and skyline for the interplay of light and shade, by means of which so much beauty is added to their ponderous masses of dark green. It is thus important in planting these hedges to have in view a definite aim which shall be fulfilled when they come to maturity.

We shall return to the subject of the yew hedge on a later page, to discuss its peculiar adaptability to the shaping and fashioning of wonderful forms which, though condemned by some garden lovers,

84   GARDENS IN THE MAKING

Fig. 21.—Hedge at Elm Tree Farm, West Wittering.

have yet endeared themselves to a greater number. Here we would emphasise the ease with which a hedge by the mere line of its planting can give a rich variety and interest to the general lay-out. We can plan the most elaborate of edifices, leaving Nature to raise the walls herself in her own time and complete our design;—and even elaboration will seldom appear overdone, for the living material itself and the quiet tones of green which pervade it will unify and harmonise all the parts and blend every detail into a reposeful whole. Square cut recesses sunk in the thickness of the hedge and spaced evenly along its length form a fine background for a lawn; others, curved on plan, range from the slightest curvature to deep cusp-like or scolloped recesses almost surrounded by the hedge itself. Broad buttresses of green can be formed on the face of the hedge, and when grown to a great height give an appearance of immense strength to these apparently massive walls. Arches can be formed, imitating a long arcade, as those surrounding the tennis lawn at Killarney (fig. 1),—a most effective treatment when enclosing a lake or pool of water. Hedges can never be of too great a thickness, for all openings will gain in appearance if they reveal a depth of feet instead of inches. The broad backs of the hedges can be cut square, sloped like a roof or rounded, or again they may be cut into massive battlements. When it is possible to look down from a height upon the walls and hedges, their thickness and any variety in plan will be grateful to the eye and will give an air of solidity and repose, which is absent from narrower lines. Stone piers with vases or projecting trees cut into shapes, placed at intervals along a tall hedge, make pleasant features, or the hedge can be planted to fill the recesses of a stone screen, or again the skyline can be diversified indefinitely with the topiary gardener's art.

It is an excellent thing at the outset to convince ourselves of the beauty and utility of walls and hedges. Such structural divisions will never be regretted, and as the years pass the choicest parts of the garden will be found within their shelter. Their beauty will grow with time, they will cultivate in us a sense of proportion, and the units of the garden being thus clearly defined they will aid us in dealing with the continual round of work. Like all things of value, they are expensive in the initial outlay; but money laid out in this way will repay itself, not once, but many times over.

Gates and Gateways

Boundaries in gardens are made for us to pass through, and the openings need only be limited by such considerations of shelter and privacy as have already been discussed. It is not necessary to furnish our openings with gates, nor, indeed, to mark them with any architectural feature. A

Fig. 22.—Wrought-iron Gateway.

simple break in wall or hedge, a tree or clipped shrub, perhaps, standing near, is all that a modest garden will require, and the choice of its situation and the size of the opening will be the chief subject of deliberation. Where, however, a little more elaboration is desired, the arch or gateway provides us with one of the most fascinating subjects in garden architecture. Whether we look across a lawn to the lofty hedge against which a broad border of flowers heaps up its bloom, or pass along a paved walk in the shelter of a high wall, it is an equal delight to see a sunlit opening to the gardens beyond, open to the eye save for a net of delicate iron scrollwork fashioned after the beautiful models of the early eighteenth century. The gateway as a symbol has always had a supreme attraction for the designer, and it is worth erecting a barrier if it gives the occasion for all the pleasure of an alluring passage through. How else shall we account for the many archways of brick and stone, and the elaborate and costly gateways hung to rich piers with sculptured finials, which are the pride of so many old-fashioned gardens? They were not a mere vain show, but were witnesses to the essential idea in the garden plan, of passing to and fro between the many mansions of the garden paradise.

Much could be written about the proportions of wrought-iron gates and of the handling of the actual design. Almost more important, however, is the treatment of the piers and their relationship to the wall itself. Piers, whether of brick or stone, or combined of both, should be sturdy enough for their work, but should also avoid an unnatural clumsiness. If they are brought well up above the wall, as in the well-known examples at Penshurst, and are crowned with a carefully designed finial, they are susceptible of the greatest refinement. The general skyline of wall and piers, if well thought out, will be seen with keen pleasure as much against the blue noonday sky as when it is outlined before the warm tones of the sunset. The gates themselves can be designed to follow the line of the wall, to rise in an arch above it, or to sink below and join the piers with a drooping curve. The first is shown in fig. 5, and the second in figs. 6 and 22 (the former based on a foreign example), while the third is suggested in the little hand-gate in fig. 20. A further alternative is to enclose the gate within an arch, as at West Wittering (see title page).

The wrought-iron gate is particularly suited to the entrance of a walled-in flower garden and to the enclosed kitchen garden, for there is an obvious sympathy between the formalism of both. In other places where the gates are omitted, it is still desirable to build piers, and these may be of many types. Built of ashlar with classic cornice and plinth, or formed of the irregular masonry of the garden wall, or again of brick, flint, or tile, they may take the usual square shape, or vary the lines by octagonal, hexagonal, or circular plans. Rusticated piers (*i.e.* those composed of projecting blocks of brick or stone) form excellent features, or the face may be panelled and enriched with carving of bold character. A sundial attached to a gate pier has a definite decorative value.

Wooden gates need careful handling in the matter of design. They are often either commonplace in conception, or—what is worse—they are bizarre and quite unrestful. The solid oak or painted door will not, of course, give any difficulty, for there are many excellent models to follow. It

Fig. 23.—Wooden Gate with Wrought-iron Panel.

is the pierced or open gate that requires care. Here, turned or square balusters will always furnish a good foundation for the design, the character of the gate being shown by the shaped top rail. A sketch of a wooden hand-gate, following an example at Cleeve Prior, will be seen in fig. 19.

The heavier types of stone and brick archways have already been illustrated. That shown on the left of the sketch of the Orangery Walk at Coombe Warren, Kingston (fig. 4), is in keeping with the architectural character of the whole scheme. The stone archway (fig. 15) is a sketch for the grounds of a large estate, while the brick gateway (fig. 14) illustrates a similar feature designed in harmony with Tudor buildings.

So far we have spoken only of individual gates, either standing alone or making a passage-way through a wall from one part of the garden to another. We must not, however, leave the subject without a word on the larger aspect of iron gates and wrought-iron screens as the principal feature of interest in gardens of some size and dignity. At the close of the seventeenth and the beginning of the eighteenth century the craft of the smith was brought to very great perfection, and magnificent compositions in ironwork were constructed as open screens sometimes as the frontispiece of the whole garden or again as a semi-background to a fine scheme of garden colour. No one who has sat for any length of time in the gardens of New College, Oxford, can forget the exquisite effect of the screen and gates which divide the College buildings from the lawns. There the plan of the advancing and recessed rails, the fine sweep of the delicate scroll-work, and the rich outline of the whole design, combine to invest the scene with an impressive beauty. Nothing enhances the effect of flower and foliage so much as this whimsical and graceful metal work, and although it is, on account of its costliness, within the reach of the few only, it is greatly to be desired that the finest product of the smith's craft should receive the encouragement and patronage which it deserves.

VI

THE DIVISIONS OF THE GARDEN

Lawns and Bowling Alleys

GREEN turf is the carpet with which we lay the broad spaces of our garden floor. Its presence near the house in an unbroken stretch is one of the most essential conditions of a reposeful and beautiful plan. Few can repel its extraordinary attraction when seen in the College gardens of Oxford or on the bowling greens of many a country seat, and its consistent beauty and texture would be a marvel to us were we less familiar with it on every countryside and over the broad downs. Yet turf is a great problem in the garden; it requires incessant labour to maintain its perfection, and its charm is easily destroyed by injudicious surroundings or by the introduction of irrelevant and disturbing features.

Its uses are very numerous. As a border it is unrivalled, and it is equally adapted to the edging of beds, paths, or buildings. The house that rises from turf appears to stand upon a level lawn, and there is no better base for the purpose of defining the contour of its plan against the ground. Turf, moreover, will allow of creepers and climbing plants growing against the house, and will prevent all untidiness. Narrow beds should be carefully avoided next the walls of a house, for they are small of content, difficult to keep in order, and they spoil the lines of the building. On the other hand, wider beds are also undesirable, for although they are beautiful in themselves, they obscure the building and carry damp to the walls. Gravel paths, too, are unsatisfactory against brick or stonework, for the materials do not harmonise and the colour generally clashes. Turf or stone paving makes the best border, the latter being akin to the architecture, and the former by its level character and fresh green colour affording a grateful contrast, besides acting as an absorbent of all damp and moisture.

Turf, then, may make our border between the house and the main paved walk or terrace, and it will be well to have grass on the outer side of the walk as well. Whether the walk is paved or gravelled, the fact that it is framed in green will greatly increase its beauty, as all will admit who are acquainted with stone flagged paths across a lawn. Where the saving of labour is not the first consideration, one cannot have too many turf-bordered paths; one may even consider the mown grass as the groundwork of the garden, from which all the other features have been cut out, and against which they are outlined. More than this, the turf itself makes most beautiful walks in dry weather, and the grass path is a thing of quite unrivalled charm. It must be kept in the very pink of perfection, soft and with the springiness of velvet, with edges trimmed with unerring straightness. These paths are often used in kitchen gardens, but they naturally will not stand a great deal of wear, so that it is advisable to have the main paths paved for the passage of the wheelbarrow. For the divisions of small formal gardens, however, grass is well suited, especially for such as are viewed from above and are not frequently entered. Shaped beds thus cut out of the green are admirable if properly enclosed with a dwarf hedge

FIG. 24.—A Turfed Enclosure.

or filling a definitely defined space (fig. 24). It is only when they are dispersed in aimless fashion about a lawn that both they and the lawn suffer from the lack of order and of any sense of design. A stretch of lawn is the better for a good background or boundary. To this fact it owes much of its beauty when close to the house or against the retaining wall of a high terrace. Unless it is flanked by gradually rising or falling ground, or a bank of trees, it should be furnished with rectilinear boundaries, or with outlines based on the curves of a geometric figure, for the eye is directed across the level area of the lawn and beyond; if, then, the immediate boundary is indefinite and characterless, the lawn itself is depreciated. In such cases a low hedge or wall, or perhaps a stone balustrade with a garden house at each end, is sufficient to give the required definition without checking the view, and the whole effect will be immeasurably improved thereby.

Whenever possible, high boundaries—formed of hedges, walls, pergolas, or lofty trees—should be given to the secondary lawns in a garden and especially to bowling greens and alleys, tennis and croquet lawns. Should they be situated, however, on terraces this is not always necessary, since the varying levels, with their banks and retaining walls, give well-defined limits—as, for example, the bowling greens at Ashdown Place (fig. 58) and Dalingridge (fig. 57), where the hedges are low. But even in such a position the enclosed lawn is an improvement from the point of view of its own appearance as apart from the general scheme, a good example being Lady Kenmare's tennis lawn at Killarney (fig. 1), which is set on the hillside, the view being preserved by the series of arches in the hedge.

One word should be added on the subject of grass banks. These are an inexpensive method of treating different levels, but they are difficult and expensive in upkeep. Moreover, if they lose their shape they easily become unsightly. It is therefore worth while, where stone or brick is procurable, to build a retaining wall, battered or sloping if preferred, from the foot and crown of which the level grass can spread.

Formal Flower Enclosures and Borders

The height of the walls or hedges which surround the formal gardens of flower beds will be

FIG. 25.—Formal Flower Beds, Killarney House, Killarney.

FLOWER ENCLOSURES AND BORDERS

determined by the size of the enclosure, for the beds must not be thrown too much in the shade. Quite low boundaries are sufficient where the garden is sheltered, so long as their outline is clear; and such formal gardens as are sunk below the level of the surrounding turf will probably need nothing more than the bank or retaining wall which marks the change in level.

The principal reason for providing formal gardens for the display of flowers, is the fact that the colour and general beauty of the blooms are intensified by their association and by massing them together. It is not, of course, necessary to shut the beds in, or to hide them from their surroundings, although the completely enclosed garden has a glory quite its own; there is room for many degrees between the box-bordered beds arranged below a friendly terrace and the high-walled rose garden with its aristocratic privacy. The effective massing of flowers is, however, common to all such arrangements, and to the same end the broad or herbaceous border should be cultivated against wall and hedge, and down the whole length of the turfed and paved walks. Each flower should appear in a profusion of its own kind, and in the deep borders or formal beds a large variety of species can be planted with room for each in abundance. A succession of brilliant colour combinations, showing all the contrasts of contour and growth, can thus be easily effected, and an occasional failure will hardly be seen. The resulting picture, whether observed from near or far, will be a vivid one, and we shall feel above all that our garden is fulfilling its purpose.

Let us suppose that we have hedged around a square plot of ground, and have provided each of its four sides with entrance gates or archways. Within the hedge we can measure off some eight to twelve feet for the border with which to surround the garden; next a flagged path, and within the square thus formed we can trace a geometrical pattern of flower beds all leading to the centre, marked by a dial, a fountain, or a lead figure. The border and the beds can be edged with box or dwarf yew, or a curb of squared stone, tile, or brick, thus keeping the walks trim and giving the design a soft but durable distinctness. With the lines thus laid we can fill the beds almost at random; the eye is satisfied with the limits set

FLOWER ENCLOSURES AND BORDERS 103

Fig. 26.—A Formal Garden and Avenue.

and does not desire formal planting or "bedding," which will overdo the effect and exhibit mere artificiality. The unrestrained growth of the flowers is attractive within the limits of the borders, although there can be no rigid law in this matter, and the taste of each gardener will have a different aim. A number of small beds can have a special colour assigned to each, and it is possible to arrange a pattern of different colours in one division. The latter, however, looks best where the flowers are such as have a soft and free growth mingling easily one with another. Do not accentuate the stiffness of stiff flowers by forming hard patterns; mingle your tulips, disperse your hyacinths, and encourage a luxuriant growth in your geraniums in pots and urns, instead of ranging these brilliant blooms in uncomfortable ranks and in an unnatural discipline.

The materials of a formal garden are thus fourfold. First, the external boundary with its gates or archways; second, the lines of stone, brick, box, or yew which trace the varied forms of the pattern; third, the filling of paving, turf, or flowers for the walks and beds; and fourth, such features as emphasise the points of the design :—a sundial, vases, standards, or cut trees and shrubs in pots. So numerous are the variations which can be played or the changes sounded with these simple instruments that it is impossible even to indicate a tithe of their potential beauties here. The simplest arrangement of rectangular beds will have its own charm, while the most intricate designs, skilfully placed, will not tire the eye, but will engage it with a rich maze of colour. A sunk garden is perhaps best laid out with quiet lines, especially if the paths are paved with stone, and if the centre is formed with a square or oblong pool of water. On the other hand, a garden enclosed by high walls or hedges needs a concentration of design and will stand much elaboration, the more so if the beds are edged with yew or box, which lend themselves to fanciful curves and re-entering angles. There are a host of formal beds and parterres which can be composed entirely of box or yew, traced in knots and labyrinths and adorned with ornaments cut from the same growth; but these belong more strictly to the topiary art, and will be described on a later page. The repetition, however, of borders one within another, as in the circles shown at St. Alban's Court (fig. 45) or in the formal patterns at Killarney (fig. 25), provides excellent material for variety, while in nowise detracting from the exhibition of the flowers.

The remarks of a former page will be found to apply to the boundary hedge and wall of the enclosed garden, but it may be added here that wherever a formal treatment is prepared in a confined space it is possible to attempt a much greater

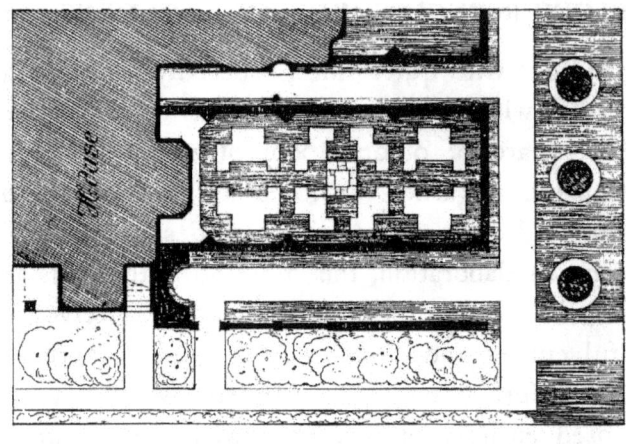
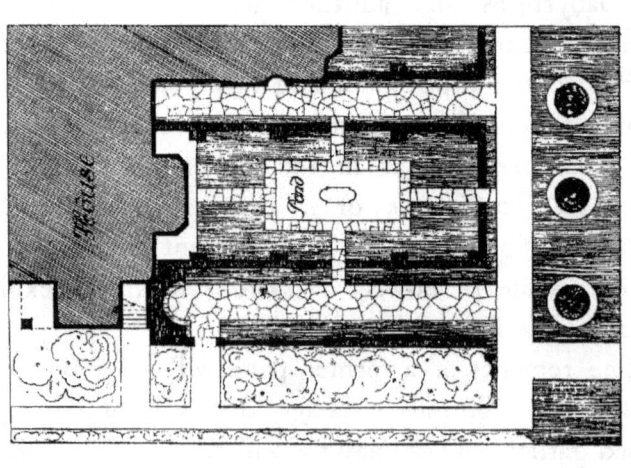

FIG. 27.—Two Designs for the Formal Garden, Ascott House.

FLOWER ENCLOSURES AND BORDERS

elaboration and to introduce more fanciful features. The top of the wall or hedge can be adorned with pinnacles or cut into grotesque figures, or again can be shaped along its whole length in a series of curves, indentations, or pierced openings. Central features or special treatments for the angles of the garden will occur to the designer, and nothing will be superfluous that adds to the sense of rarity and richness that should pervade the almost sacred enclosure.

Once the formal treatment of flower beds is appreciated it will be found to be the simplest and most effective method of display, and its application to every part of the garden will present no difficulty. Waste space in a garden should be an unknown quantity, and as long as there is sunlight and air the most irregular figure will yield to the formal treatment and provide a home for flowers. We must, of course, avoid, from practical considerations, too great a proximity between our flower beds and the trunks and roots of trees. Yet we shall do well to remember the immense value of forest tree and thick shrub, which by their association with the boundaries of the enclosed gardens give them a new beauty, add to their respose, and make an effective contrast with their playful formalism and exactitude. The formal rose beds at Dalingridge (fig. 32) are greatly enhanced by the trees of the wild garden beyond and the azalea hedge to the left. If trees are lacking some other feature—a terrace wall, an orangery, a garden house or dovecot—will perhaps provide the anchorage which is such a grateful element in the design. But no such help is needed where clean and close-cut divisions of yew rise from the perfect level of turf as at Penshurst, forming as effective a frame and background as could be desired to the brilliant gaiety of the flowers. Looking out from the windows of those stately galleries we could wish for no other form than that presented with so much skill. The flowers do not lose, but even gain in brilliance, while these geometrical borderings make us remember that they bloom on the estate of an ancient manor, and express the delightful unity and kinship between the old walls and the renewed life of the summer flowers. The function of the formal garden may thus be the most valuable in the whole range of garden-craft.

Fig. 28.—Formal Garden, Elm Tree Farm, West Wittering.

Paving and its Uses

In the paved walk beauty meets utility, and when skilfully devised neither can claim precedence. Nothing makes the garden so serviceable as the paths and terraces on which you can always walk dry-shod; nothing, on the other hand, is more restful and beautiful in our garden architecture than the flagged ways across its turf or between the deep borders of its flowers. Stone, quarried as it is from the native hillside, is the material most readily assimilated by the garden scheme, and trees, flowers, grass, and fern all find that their colours harmonise with its pale and neutral tints. As durable as picturesque, not more useful than pleasing, the roughly jointed slabs of stone always remind us that they are the natural product of the soil itself, and are sure to be growingly responsive to the softening influences of the weather and the years.

Many as are the forms of paving and diverse as the materials can be, nothing will excel the hard stone flags which are quarried in various parts of the country, the best being of Yorkshire stone or from the famous Isle of Purbeck. But paving-bricks and tiles are excellent in certain situations, especially in covered or shaded walks, and in loggias and summer houses. We must beware, however, of tiles with a glazed surface—those in common use being distinguished only by their utter unsuitability to the garden both as regards their texture and colour. The ordinary red quarries, 6, 9, or 12 inches square, should be chosen, for their surface is rough enough to give a firm foothold, and their colour—a deep and quiet red—is not discordant among the bright and mingled tints of Nature. A very durable but rather expensive form of paving can be made of roofing tiles set on edge in cement; these tiles are useful when mingled with brick or stone, and they can be easily formed into simple geometric figures—much as the Romans used to employ their tiles to reinforce their concrete. They lend themselves to any shape, and are particularly effective when they are made to describe circles or to trace a variety of curved outlines.

Stone paving may be laid with roughly squared flags or with broken stone of irregular shapes pieced together like a puzzle. The surroundings will generally give the key to the form which may best be employed. The squared stone looks more in keeping with strictly architectural features or in paths across a level lawn, the random type being best in irregular areas or within less severe boundaries. When squared stone is used it is as well to break joint as much as possible; but if some joints are to follow through — *i.e.* when several stones adjoin one another with their edges in a direct line—let these joints be at right angles to

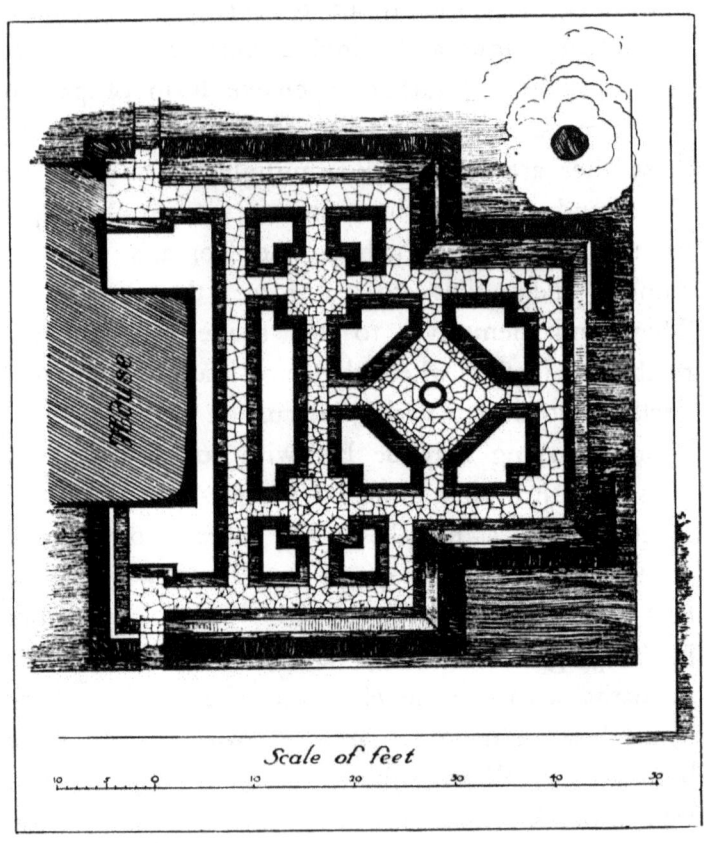

Fig. 29.—Formal Garden, Henley Hall.

with the altered conditions of the open air,—but in some carefully selected court or on a terrace where the sun is a constant visitor, we may essay a composition wherein bright colours—fine blues and greens mingled with white—form the keynote of the design. Normally, however, the quiet, rough, serviceable materials of stone and brick will be found the most friendly to the purpose we have in view.

Paving is the ideal method of treating practically all paths in a garden, although considerations of cost will generally confine its use to certain limits. Gravelled paths are not so dry or durable, and, more than this, they lack the beautiful tone and picturesque jointing of the stone flags. The colour of gravel is never really welcome in the garden picture, and any extent of it is apt to put all else out of harmony. It cannot be compared with stone when used across a lawn or next to strips of turf.

Every garden is the better for a liberal allowance of paving. It is required in many places, and forms the most effective embroidery to garden architecture, providing, as it does, a groundwork which makes each feature blend with its surroundings. Orangeries the longest direction of path, or terrace. In a path, for instance, it does not matter how many joints reach in a line from side to side, but care should be taken to break all joints running the same way as the path itself. In a broad terrace it will be found advisable to select stones which are roughly of the same size for the outside edges and to fill the central area with the extremes of large and small slabs.

The insertion of simple geometric patterns in a slightly different type of stone, and all natural and haphazard methods of introducing colour and variety such as millstones, bands of brick and tile, etc., furnish matters of pleasant experiment. Tesselated pavements, parti-coloured glazed tiles or mosaic should be very rarely used save in specially designed surroundings, and then only with the greatest discretion. It is not that the brilliant colours of these materials are unable to blend with those of sky and flower, but rather that our English climate does not favour the effects which are common to Southern Countries, and we are therefore largely unpractised in the art. The decorative methods of within doors lose their meaning when brought into competition

FIG. 30.—Formal Garden, Ascott House.

(fig. 4), garden houses, statuary, even balustrades and steps, look isolated and artificial unless one can lead up to them with a square of paving or a stone path. Pools with paved margins, seats with stone platforms, gateways with broad stone thresholds all look the better for its ministration. But chiefly it is valuable against the house itself,—for a stretch of paving, as at Dalingridge (fig. 10) or West Wittering (fig. 56), adds immensely to the restfulness and dignity of the building. Spaces between projecting wings, verandahs, loggias, and other recesses or specially defined areas, call for a paved floor, and are improved if the stone is extended beyond them to link them with the garden itself. Particularly is paving adapted to the enclosed garden, the small quadrangle, cloistered court, or to the confined garden of the town house, where both grass and flowers are difficult to rear. In such enclosures the stone path will be the basis of the design, and in its shape and arrangement will lie the interest and charm of the whole idea. It is a subject that allows of infinite elaboration, and the designer need have no fear of exhausting the devices to which it lends itself, alone or in combination with other features.

Very much will depend on the method of laying the stone, which can be easily made to look either commonplace or unnaturally odd. In water gardens and in certain quiet walks it is permissible to leave wide cracks and broken angles for small flowers and rock plants to flourish. But, as a rule, it is well to avoid making our path a flower bed, and our paving should be justified by its own beauty without extreme precision or obvious defects. As in other things, the mean is the best course,—extremes will not give us a lasting satisfaction or permanent pleasure.

VII

THE TERRACED GARDEN

Terraces and Balustrades

THE term "terrace" has come to be applied more particularly to a walk or platform which is raised above the surrounding country, but in a broader sense it may serve to describe any piece of ground which has been levelled and defined in relation to a building or other important feature or part of the garden. It forms an essential part of the general scheme as outlined in these pages and, as we have already pointed out, its chief function is to give stability to the whole design, correcting awkward levels, affording the stage or platform for architectural features, and generally providing the base or axial lines on which the entire lay-out depends.

The treatment of the terrace will not, of course, be the same in every position, but it will usually retain at least one open side, where the boundary

TERRACES AND BALUSTRADES

will be kept low and the view left uninterrupted. It is essentially a place of prospect, open to the air and sky, although it may often be prolonged into sheltered walks and covered ways. The potentiality of the terrace as a subject for design is very great, and in the past it has provided the opportunity for widely varied types of arrangement. As an outdoor "room" it can be paved and furnished with seats and every variety of garden furniture and ornament. As a platform or place of vantage from which to enjoy the view, it requires the help of a retaining wall crowned with balustrading, a parapet of brick or stone, a low hedge, or a fence curiously contrived of wrought-iron. Such features combined with a flight of steps to a lower level can be made into a delightful composition as viewed from below. Again, prolonged as a walk, the terrace may lead the eye to a beautiful vista, through trees, or over lawns, up or down the sloping ground, to a distant view on one hand or terminating in a garden house on the other.

Once we have set out the lines of our main terrace and pondered upon its possibilities laterally and at each end, we shall find that the rest will largely take care of itself and fall into line.

Fig. 31.—Terrace Balustrading

On a sloping site it is important that the ground immediately adjacent to the house should be levelled to a sufficient distance from the building to give it stability and restfulness. The whole of this depth need not necessarily be given up to the paved terrace, but part can be occupied by lawn as at Dalingridge (fig. 10). An overdose of paving or gravel on the garden side is rather apt to remind us of the entrance courtyard, without its dignity. In point of fact our efforts should be directed towards making the paved terrace when adjacent to the house as welcome and habitable as possible for sitting out of doors. On a steep slope where the level platform

and Garden House.

is small we can easily achieve this result, for the balustrade or parapet will frame the terrace, and since it will be separated from the remainder of the garden by its elevation, we shall be compelled to furnish it to make it attractive. There is no reason, however, why we should not repeat the treatment on a level site by marking off a reasonable area with a low balustrade or hedge and adorning it with seats and tubs or urns for choice flowers and dwarf trees. The outlook from this terrace is much the same as from the house itself, and if we have taken infinite care and thought in providing walks, avenues, and good views of our lawns and flower gardens from the windows, we shall enjoy them equally from the outdoor apartment thus prepared.

Beyond our main terrace will be others, arranged as far as possible to provide the best standpoints to view the gardens. On the single slope of a hillside our whole garden may have perforce to be a succession of terraces broken here and there by a planted slope, a line of trees, or a bank too steep to level. Such a garden is expensive in its groundwork and walling, but if well carried out it may be made a veritable enchantment. Here is an opportunity of blending the formal treatment with a complete abandonment to Nature; stone balustrades linked to archways and summer houses can alternate with retaining walls covered with creepers and bushes. Here and there the terraces can be taken some considerable length, at other places they will be broken by deep hollows in the side of the hill, dells filled with trees, undergrowth, bracken and fern. Such a garden effectively conceals the art by which it is produced; it does no violence to Nature, but reinforces her own untamed beauty and brings it all within the reach of our enjoyment.

In some situations the terrace *motif* can be over-

Fig. 32.—Terrace Wall and Rose Garden, Dalingridge Place.

done, and where the gradient of the ground is not very steep it will be advisable to accept the slope, and correct it only at intervals where a level walk seems most desirable. Terraced walks are appropriately placed round sunk gardens, pools, and lawns for tennis or bowls, or they may follow the line of a fine wall separated only by the proper width for an herbaceous border. Wherever they are found they will promote the most commonplace lines to an appearance of dignity and beauty. Moreover, the key to the treatment of many a difficult and apparently hopeless site is to be found in cutting a terrace right through the troublesome area, which soon is brought from chaos into order.

The stone balustrade is by far the most beautiful finish to the retaining wall of the terrace, but it has suffered at the hand of many a caricaturist and traducer, and its reputation has been much tarnished thereby. Let the balustrade, however, be in good freestone with its surface left somewhat rough; let the balusters themselves be of good pattern, full in outline and sturdy in design, and let them be placed well apart with more than their own width between them; and finally, let the stone rail or coping which covers them be low in section but broad in its width. These conditions fulfilled, you will not regret your choice. A balustrade looks at its best when seen from below with the sky behind it; then the advantage of the wide spacing is evident and the quality of the shape of each baluster tells. If you have a deeply sunk garden with a walk at the end at a considerable altitude above it, crown the retaining wall with these stone balusters and your garden will gain instant charm. Avoid square-turned balusters set close together, and be sparing in ornaments placed above the stone rail. A flat level character is the best to seek,—the stone piers should be wide and of the same height as the balusters; and if diversity is desired, it should be sought in variations in *plan*, with curves and re-entering angles arranged in the wall itself.

A low terrace wall (some sixteen inches high, a comfortable height if used as a seat) can be treated in a variety of ways, while lengths of plain unpierced walling alternating with one or two balusters give a very pleasing effect. Some difficulty may be experienced in giving a satisfactory finish to a balustrade when it does not terminate against a

Fig. 33.—Terrace Wall and Flagged Path.

building or a higher wall. A length of solid wall, with a stone vase, or a long scroll-shaped console carved in stone will provide a simple solution.

There are many interesting forms of balustrading that can be made of brick and tile work, pierced strapwork and simple geometric designs being fairly easily arranged with shaped tiles. Miniature arcades after the Jacobean manner can be formed in stone, and if not cut with too much precision will harmonise well with a building of Tudor or Early Renaissance character. In all these types it is important that the designs should be simple, the shapes easily grasped, and the material not too hard,

TERRACES AND BALUSTRADES

nor the workmanship too precise for the conditions which we have laid down for garden architecture.

Before leaving the subject of the terrace and garden walk it is necessary to touch for a moment on the subject of the projecting terrace. It is often of value to bring out a kind of promontory at right angles to the main walk, as a pier projects into the sea, to screen some part of the garden or to afford a special standpoint for a view. Such features have already been referred to at Dalingridge (fig. 10) and Ashdown Place (fig. 58). A simpler application of the same principle will be found in the bastion-like projections which can be made along the length of a terrace, diversifying its outline and giving interest to its wall and balustrade. Variation in plan is of the utmost importance in all garden design, and where terraces are concerned such innovations will be found of great value. Along a broad walk, too, the bastion-like projections in hedge or wall will give a gradation and scale, beside a pleasant variety, to the whole design. The occurrence and shape of these features will depend upon their situation, but it will seldom be found that a garden can do entirely without them.

Steps and Stairways

Changing levels constitute the garden's cadence, and the steps and stairways form the bridge by which we descend from the highest to the lowest notes of its song. It is not enough for us to terrace the hillside or plant the valley—we must make the communications between them, and thanks to the limitations of the human footstep the size of each stair is fairly constant and becomes a valuable unit of scale in garden architecture. A flight of steps is a graduated walk, broken at regular intervals by the vertical and horizontal planes; it is thus a place of light and shadow; it suggests, moreover, the poetry of motion, and yet remains a stationary link between an upper and a lower stage; perhaps its chief delight lies in its open invitation to ascend or descend, and its promise of a changing view and varying prospect.

Yet, in spite of its essentially attractive qualities, and although its potential beauty as an architectural composition can scarcely be rivalled, the stairway is commonly treated as of little account in the garden, as though it were an object of mere utilitarian purpose and not worth a moment's thought as to its shape, size, colour, or position. None of these points should be neglected; the shape of step and balustrade should be graceful and quiet in outline; the size, both in width and general proportions, should be suited to the parts of the garden which the stair unites; the materials should be chosen with due regard to colour and texture; and above all, the position of the steps should be selected with the greatest care.

There are two general points which it is helpful to bear in mind when arranging garden steps. The first is that where the steps are few in number they should be given as great a width as possible, while conversely, where there are a great number of steps they will look well if proportionately narrow. There is a natural compensation between those two dimensions of a stairway which require the width and length to vary inversely; and although there may be a number of exceptions, the above will be found a good working rule in the majority of cases. The second point is that the appearance of a stairway is greatly improved if it is buttressed by some prominent feature at its side. Take your steps

Fig. 34.—Terrace Stairway.

down by a group of trees, a high wall, or yew hedge; plant a holly alongside, or lead them beside a building or the projecting "bastion" of a terrace; wherever it is possible, group your steps with some outstanding mass of foliage or architecture and you will find their charm increased immeasurably. Most garden features are improved by association with one another, but stairways are particularly in need of the companionship of a protecting neighbour.

Unless an elaborate architectural composition is attempted—and even this requires its proper theatre—an isolated flight of steps will need great care to look well. In such a position a low block of masonry or brickwork, or a cube of cut yew on each side, will give it an anchorage, or we must try to strengthen it by a wide parapet kept low and skilfully turned or built into a square of paving which will bind the steps to the ground and make them look as if they have grown in their present position.

Let us consider the steps which are suited to three different situations :—first, the descent from a walk or terrace of some size and dignity, where the architectural treatment requires some elaboration. Second, the descent from lawn to lawn, or from one garden to another, where the difference of level is not great, and where the positions for steps will often vary. And third, steps in random paving, and those informal and long stairways which will climb the wooded glade or the slope of the wild garden and the " wilderness."

First, then, with regard to the more elaborate structures. Provided there is some little depth, the descent from a terrace may be made into a composition of great beauty and dignity. The steps can be led down in two broad flights, turning in opposite directions to unite below, or may unite on a central platform and then turn to land at separate points. With fine balustrades, statuary, or vases to mark the sweeping curves or returning flights, the most remarkable effects can be obtained. The retaining wall between the twin stairways, or flanking them, will dominate the composition with the level lines of its balustrade, and below a fountain or pool can divide the approaching or receding steps and introduce a new element of charm. Innumerable types, with the same underlying principle, can be devised from the most elaborate subjects for sculpture to the modest double flight in brick and tile. They all depend on the balance obtained by the repetition of features, and their variety is made possible by the nature of the stairway and the ease with which it is turned in every direction to suit the fancy. In all such examples the architectural detail, however simple, should be well chosen and handled, for the most excellent scheme and the most ingenious fancy are quickly ruined by an unskilful interpretation.

Fig. 35.—Steps to Bowling Green, Ashdown Place.

The second group of stairways may be described best by referring to the illustrations. The sketch of Ashdown Place (fig. 35) shows a useful method of descending from one terrace to another where it is desired to avoid the sharp vertical boundary of the retaining wall. The steps are arranged in pairs with turf levels between them, and their great breadth preserves the open character. Fig. 34 shows an isolated descent from a terrace through a deep herbaceous border. The flowers on either side give a kind of moral support to the steps, and the vases with cut trees relieve the comparative poverty which would otherwise be inseparable from so small a feature. A similar service is rendered by the clumps of grasses which are shown in fig. 21 on a simple grass bank, but the finest supporters on either side of a broad flight of steps are undoubtedly to be found in Irish yews, trimmed or untrimmed, standing like giant sentinels outlined against the sky. As a rule it is better to arrange the stairway at each end of a terrace or series of terraces rather than in the centre, since the stair provides an interesting architectural finish or flanking feature, as well as being rendered more effective in itself by this position, where it has the support of a wall or something that serves the same purpose. Sometimes the terrace wall will terminate under trees or against planting, and here some curved steps around a circular landing—the upper concave and the lower convex—will be found both convenient and picturesque, as in the example from Dalingridge Place (fig. 36), where the stairway lies under the shadow of a fine azalea hedge of irregular shape.

Wherever the stairway is not treated in a strictly architectural way with stone balusters, vases and figures, we should guard against too finished a surface to the stonework. Steps by themselves without architectural detail should appear to be formed from the ground itself, and should be roughly jointed and not rigidly level. They can be curved in plan and made to assume a number of different shapes, but in all this they should keep an air of simplicity and a restfulness in outline, with low stone walls and piers to give them balance and substance. The old efforts towards "rustic" masonry were based on a misconception of the true method of modifying architecture to harmonise with nature. They resulted only in producing irregular forms

Fig. 36.—Circular Steps, Dalingridge Place.

which were as far away from natural beauty as the most conventional of architectural features, and they were composed of materials which refused to surrender themselves to the action of wind and weather. As we have said before, the forms should be simple, decorous, and well-defined, for only by the careful choice of a material and surface which will not withstand the hand of time may we hope to modify their artificiality and allow Nature to effect her conquest.

STEPS AND STAIRWAYS

The foregoing remarks apply with particular emphasis to the last group among the stairways which we have enumerated—those formed in walks laid with broken flags and up wooded and secluded slopes where the foliage is partly cultivated or wholly wild. Nothing will suit such positions better than steps composed of flat stones, with irregular open joints and having as deep a tread and as low a rise as possible. If the stones themselves are some four inches thick, their front edges can be roughly undercut to hold the shadow which looks so well in an ascent of many steps; as a rule, however, paving stones will be about two inches in thickness, each step being formed of two stones, the upper of which may overhang the lower and give the required depth of shadow. The degree of steepness in the slope will determine the number of steps and how far these will have to be in one or many flights, or perhaps divided into groups of threes and fours. Such steps will often not require a parapet, but can finish against a bank of flowers or ferns, or an irregular line of stones arranged as a curb.

The parapet or retaining wall for steps forms too large a subject for detailed treatment here, but it may be said in general that a low flight is better with a solid wall, while the open balustrade is at its best when high enough to show sky and foliage between its stonework. The sloping balustrade is not invariably satisfactory, and it can be replaced in a variety of ways. Perhaps one of the simplest is to carry out the side walls enclosing the steps at the level of the top step, since a stairway always looks well between walls, especially when the latter are not carried higher than the upper ground level. A few steps with a curving parapet wall is an excellent device to turn the direction of a path, and an upward flight of stairs, even if only two or three, will give point and interest to a long walk when seen from a distance. There is, indeed, no end to the usefulness in our garden design of the simple feature of the stairway, and its value is not in any way impaired whether it is treated with economy or with a fine disregard of cost and a single eye to its effect.

VIII

GARDEN FURNITURE AND BUILDINGS

Seats and Arbours

THE garden seat might claim almost the sole monopoly of the term garden furniture were it not that many adornments, which exist only for display, have become included within the title. The seat, however, is the one piece of inevitable furniture which is indispensable to any and every garden; and since it has to perform the same function as its cousins in the hall and drawing-room, and yet at the same time must be in tune with the scheme of outdoor life, it will readily be seen that its design merits some careful consideration.

Perhaps the most widespread mistake in regard to garden seats is that they are made too light for

Fig. 37.—Oak Seat, Pitchford Hall.

permanent use without doors and for their proper harmony with the walls and hedges of a garden, and at the same time too heavy for easy transportation into the shelter of the house. It must always be remembered that light furniture, such as cane or deck chairs, can be brought out whenever the summer weather invites us to rest beneath the open sky. The fixed garden seat does not enter into competition with these instruments of ease and idleness; it is there for other reasons, and the conditions of its existence being more rigorous, it must be designed and fashioned on more permanent lines. Moreover, as a fixed feature of the garden it must have its architectural character; its platform or shelter must be specially prepared for it, and its position must be chosen with due regard to the design of the garden, and must have nothing of haphazard in the way it is placed.

In common with practically all things in the garden scheme, position is the most important thing to determine first. The seat must be put in the right and desirable place for use, and this place must be also made appropriate to the design. The necessity for seats, therefore, should not be overlooked when we begin to outline the general idea of the garden, and success in this detail will depend upon the appearance of purpose thus obtained. All open terraces provide excellent situations for seats; they can be arranged in recesses in the walls, either at regular intervals or grouped in a projecting "bastion" or platform where such features exist. These projections will be especially valuable where the terrace looks upon a good view, for since the seat must not have its back to the prospect it is important to be able to place it at right angles to the walk, where the seats can be in pairs facing one another. Another, and one of the most charming of the many positions available, is at the end of a terrace or long walk. Here the treatment will depend upon whether the seat closes the vista or whether the end of the walk gives upon a further view. In the latter case the seats can be at each side as described above, within such dwarf hedges as are shown at the end of the bowling greens at Dalingridge (fig. 10) and Ashdown Place (fig. 58). In the former they should face the walk, and be backed by a shaped hedge or wall and supported, perhaps, on either side by dwarf piers, vases, or pots with cut trees to give them some little distinction.

Although an open situation (with a proper background and setting) is desirable for the seat, yet there are innumerable places in the garden plan which invite some means for resting and enjoying the beauty of the scene at leisure. On lawns, in enclosed gardens, beneath the shade of a fine tree, or in some secluded part of the wild garden, the desire

SEATS AND ARBOURS

Fig. 38.—Circular Seat, Ascott House.

will be felt. No one looks upon an unsheltered seat as serviceable in all weathers, but as long as it is built well and strongly framed it will serve its purpose in the proper season. It is important, however, that a good platform should be provided, of paving preferably, to ensure a dry situation. Seats require some attention, too, in keeping them clean and in good condition, and unless they are of oak or teak they should be painted every second year.

It is often possible to devise some shelter which shall not rise to the rank of a garden house and yet will not rob the seat of its own character. An

Fig. 39.—A painted Seat.

arched recess in a wall is shown in fig. 40, and an open recess can be roofed with interlacing timbers, pergola-fashion, to form an arbour (fig. 3). In fig. 44 a niche in a yew hedge answers the same purpose, and treillage lends itself admirably to a similar treatment. In such cases care should be exercised in keeping the interior swept and clean, leaving the outside to be covered by the random growth of creepers or climbing roses, or by the trimmed outlines of the yew.

The material to be used and the type of design to be selected for seats is a somewhat vexed question,

SEATS AND ARBOURS

It is the rule rather than the exception to see the inappropriate thing in both cases.

The stone seat is naturally less adapted for use, as the material is not so dry and clean as wood. Yet it undoubtedly harmonises more easily with the garden picture. The chief point to observe is the importance of linking a stone seat with its immediate surroundings. However ornate and beautiful in itself, it will be in danger of looking like an exhibit in the grounds of a museum if it is not properly buttressed by wall, hedge, or other sufficient feature. Where there is a curved wall of brick or stone, or low piers with balustrading, the simple stone slab set some sixteen inches high will look perfectly natural and unaffected. Link it with the structural lines of the garden whenever possible, and if it must stand by itself prolong the seat at each end to form a dwarf stone wall and finish with stone tubs for small trees or flowers.

Wooden seats are not really less dependent on their surroundings, but being more obviously a type of furniture, and being numerous on account of their greater usefulness, they are susceptible of a wider freedom in design. Hard woods such as oak and teak are the best materials, whether left with their natural colour or painted, but selected deal or pine if frequently painted is quite serviceable. Trellis of interlacing or jointed bars, from its long association with garden architecture, will provide the best types of design for the backs, and some care should be taken to obtain lines of sufficient strength, beauty, and comfort in the legs, arms, and rails. The seats at Ascott (fig. 38), Pitchford Hall (fig. 37), and those shown in figs. 39 and 33, give some suggestions of varying size.

Loggias and Garden Houses

The garden shelter, under which we may include verandahs, loggias, garden houses, summer houses, and temples, presents a subject of the utmost importance to those who desire to make their garden really useful, and at the same time to give it the completeness and the architectural finish which it undoubtedly requires. Of the usefulness of these shelters it would seem almost unnecessary to speak, were it not for the general reluctance to devote sufficient thought and money to them. The loggia and the verandah tempt us from the rooms of the house

LOGGIAS AND GARDEN HOUSES

Fig. 40.—Seat in a Brick Recess.

and invite us to view the garden and to feel the sweetness of the air; the garden house persuades us to go further, and to walk at least as far as its shelter. Without either, the hospitality of the garden is impaired at those times when its influence might be most refreshing although the weather conditions may be uninviting. Moreover, in the more distant enclosures the garden house is the representative as it were of the main building, and is a sign of our occupation. Nothing furnishes a garden more completely than a well-designed summer house;

nothing impresses so much upon one the feeling that the owner and his friends *live* here, and like to rest among the flowers and foliage. This is not a merely fanciful suggestion, but is part of the whole presentation of the garden plan as discussed in these pages. It is part of the principle that the garden should bear the stamp of design in every detail, that it should not be a forced imitation of Nature, but the product of man's own love of carefully considered and ordered effect, and that it should be fully equipped for his use and possession. It is the plea of the architect for garden-architecture,—a plea which, however much it may be discounted by its source, is yet, we think, amply justified in practice.

We have already referred in passing to the value of such garden buildings in close proximity to the house, to their usefulness in wedding the house to the garden and in affording a better scenic background for the general design. The Elizabethan practice of a raised terrace with a "banqueting house" at each end is capable of much variety and charm, and is a surprising addition to the pleasure to be derived from our domain. Indeed, the garden

Fig. 41.—A Garden House.

house has a curiously close relationship with the terrace, wherever it may be placed; and whether seen at the end of a paved walk or from the lower levels over which it appears raised as an integral portion and a crowning feature of the retaining wall (fig. 31), it is sure to make an admirable composition. Whether square, circular, or many-sided on plan, its bulk is usually a rough cube, and its steep conical or pyramidal roof always provides a welcome feature. With the trees and gateways it breaks the skyline and dominates the scene in which it is placed.

The essential requirements of a garden house are few and simple, yet they are capable of a very wide diversity of treatment. From the timber buildings, taking their inspiration from the mediæval period, to the prim and quaint essays in miniature classical architecture which were the joy of the eighteenth century, we can draw on a very extensive choice. As long as we avoid the extremes of too great a finish or too obvious a "rusticity," and make the outline simple and the detail good, we cannot go far astray. The architects of the time of James I. possessed perhaps the greatest felicity in this kind of design, the playfulness of Jacobean detail being subservient to quiet modelling, while the mouldings and carving were kept broad and even coarse,—to be softened but not obliterated by time. Pyramidal tile or lead roofs (figs. 31 and 41) are generally the best; but even here there is scope for much fancy, and an oak lantern with a vane forms a pretty terminal. Two enclosed garden houses are shown in figs. 41 and 42, the former having a sheltered verandah before it, both being definitely architectural in design. Another type is shown in the two designs for a garden shelter at Ascott, each being arranged as an alcove for a seat at the end of a broad walk. In that in fig. 18 the roof is supported by columns, but in fig. 3 the main structure is a semicircular wall faced with tiles and crowned with a balustrade, shaded by open timbers for climbing roses.

The close connection between these little buildings and the garden walls is seen in numerous old examples, where the roofs of the former add a seeming stability to the brick and stonework of the latter, and give to them an additional beauty. The river wall which divided the Thames from the old-time gardens along its northern bank from the

Fig. 42.—Another Garden House.

Temple to Chelsea was studded with similar buildings, and their effectiveness in the angles of a courtyard, the sides of a formal flower garden, or the ends of walk and terrace, should bring them back into favour. The present generation is regaining some of the past skill in picturesque grouping and is reviving those artless lines of beauty, which despite their seemingly accidental effect are really the result of much thought. But it will not be until the *need* for the garden house and its type of buildings has really returned that we shall get back to the peculiar charm of the seventeenth and eighteenth century garden. The art of the past lapsed into artificiality and then passed away, and now we have to regret that we impatiently discarded too much of the old spirit, and lost the good with the bad.

Greenhouses and Orangeries

The rival æsthetic schools which counsel us on the one hand to hide all useful things where "appearances" count, and on the other to expose them on the assumption that real usefulness connotes beauty, need not seriously trouble us. To the plain man there are many things of utility which are not easily brought into harmony with his ideas of what is lovely to look upon, and yet to the artist the ugly and useful thing tempts him to try and fashion it anew. The problem is no small one at times, and it is certainly not an easy one in the case of hothouses, where the expanse of glass rebels against any attempt to coax it into line with the architecture of either house or garden.

In large grounds there will be ample space for

glass in connection with the kitchen gardens (see fig. 60), and where it is customary to raise choice flowers in long ranges of hothouses, these can be in a properly defined area screened at the end by treillage or walls through which the visitor can enter and pass through each house. The difficulty becomes a real one when the greenhouse is attached to the house itself, as must often be the case in small property and wherever there is a desire to have plants under glass approached from the rooms. Many attempts have been made to " beautify " these buildings, often at the expense of their utility and more frequently at the expense of good taste. The safest course to pursue is to avoid ornament, to build the greenhouse in as straightforward and substantial a manner as possible, and then to plan its immediate surroundings with the greatest care. If it is treated as a *lacuna* in the scheme of solid buildings and walls, and is kept quite simple, it will scarcely assert itself. Set between formal walls, and behind a dwarf hedge or paving with square tubs, it will fall into line with the general plan.

It is quite different with orangeries and bay houses. Here the glass can be arranged in long

Georgian windows, and the fronts of these buildings afford one of the most inviting opportunities for garden architecture. The sketch of Mr. Devey's orangery at Coombe Warren (fig. 4) shows an end treatment, but the length of these buildings as a background to a formal garden or broad terrace is quite ideal, and will bear the presence of fairly elaborate detail.

IX

SOME OLD-WORLD FEATURES

Arcaded Walks and Pergolas

WHETHER or not the "pensile or hanging gardens of Babylon" were an early form of pergola, there is good reason for believing that the most primitive types of gardening included the raising of timber frames for the support of climbing plants. And the love of the ancients for the simple architecture of the colonnade would suggest their familiarity with this beautiful method of guiding foliage and displaying bloom. The "alleys" of mediæval and later days were also often enclosed about with a framework for roses, for well these lovers of gardens knew that their riotous luxuriance could not be better shown than on the formal lines of post and crossbar.

The pergola is garden architecture *par excellence*; it is not architecture in the garden, nor garden products superimposed upon architecture — it is the simplest form of construction completely conquered and possessed by plant and flower. Yet it retains the qualities of architecture — the strength, stability, and rhythm which proceed from regularity in setting out, simplicity in design, and the repetition of its ordered parts. It follows, then, that the pergola can perform a most useful part in promoting the marriage between house and garden, it carries a structural significance with it, and wherever it can be schemed as an appendage or prolongation of the building itself it is of great value. This quality in the pergola makes it important that it should not stand alone; like other garden features, it requires connection with the salient lines of the design, and more than they, it needs either a definite point of departure, or a termination in a wall, garden house, or gateway. It forms a light and beautiful substitute for a building, wall, or cloistered walk, wherever a lawn or terrace calls for such a background, and its height and shadowed recesses give an air of shelter and privacy in positions which otherwise would lie too open or form too flat a picture. If a long path traverses several enclosures in one line, it is worth while forming a pergola over one section of its length, beginning and ending with a boundary; for without disturbing the direction of the walk it breaks the distance and diversifies the vista.

The variety of situations in which a pergola may fittingly be placed, is rivalled only by the number of types and methods by which it may be constructed. Leaning against a lofty wall or crossing the open court, enclosing a formal garden or built on a terraced hillside, descending by steps the gentle gradient of a sloping garden or surrounding, in a circular or many-sided figure, the walls of some cool retreat, in all these and many more positions it will be found appropriate and useful. And as to its materials and form, we can almost select at pleasure. The nearer the house, the more solid and architectural should be the construction, although the heavier types need by no means be confined to this position. The horizontal supports for the foliage will, of course, be of wood; and where heavy beams are used, the standards should be built of solid piers of a generous size. Old stone columns, if procur-

ARCADED WALKS AND PERGOLAS 159

Fig. 43.—A Timbered Pergola.

able, are excellent; but stout piers of stone, brick, or tile if built with raked-out joints look very well, especially if varied in plan, square alternating with round or hexagonal sections. Where timber is used for the posts as well as the flat roof, we can use all the devices of the old mediæval carpenter, and should not neglect his rules. The appearance as well as the reality of strength is needed, and timbers must never "sag" but rather curve upwards, and braces, struts, and dragon-ties may be employed to bind and beautify the structure (fig. 43). In this way quite light material can be effectively converted into a useful pergola, and larch poles properly braced, with an interlacing trellis above, will answer perfectly where the surroundings do not demand a more solid erection.

The colonnaded and flat-roofed pergola is first cousin to the arcaded walk. The latter, the arched form of which is more easily built with light iron hoops, is adapted to the narrowest as well as the widest of paths; and the series of arches when connected by stout wire, forms a veritable tunnel over which can be trained all manner of climbing plants or fruit trees. Such features are the essence of a garden, they are the concentration of flower and fruit in such general assemblage as shall enchant the sight, and whether viewed from within or without are equally a treasure-house of charm, "an infinite varietie of sweet smelling flowers, colouring not onely the earth, but decking the ayre and sweetning every breath and spirit." Those words not here attempt to arbitrate between the two opposing tastes, but shall frankly confess our delight in these "children's" toys, asking the graver sort among our readers to overlook our weakness with a kind indulgence.

We share with by far the greater number of the gardeners of old time the love of all that is fanciful and picturesque, provided that the materials thereof and their method and disposition are in full harmony with the garden atmosphere. Our art is akin to the making of poetry, which in its lyric moods is beautified by quaint conceits, and in its epic passages is peopled by heroic forms and structures of strange and fairy type. We set out to make of our garden a palace of delights, and the more the imagination is stimulated by these simple variations in mass and outline the more completely do we attain the end in view.

The appropriateness of using such close-growing foliage as box and yew in fashioning the decorative features of the formal garden does not lie wholly in the facility with which they can be clipped and trained. It is the fact that they are of the very growth of the garden, and that in colour and texture of William Lawson, who wrote in the reign of King James I., tell us what the English gardeners of an earlier period felt; and why should we, who surely love our flowers no less, discard the beautiful old-fashioned methods of display? Let us have wide pergolas and long arcaded walks, circular temples and pillars for roses, and let us not fear that Nature will fail to dress them with beauty, nor that in her luxuriance she will show herself ungrateful for the support and guidance of our formal craftsmanship. If we lead she will follow; but if we fail to give her the opportunities she had of old, only ours will be the loss.

Topiary and the Labyrinth

In his terse way, Lord Bacon dismissed the art of the topiary gardener when he wrote: "I, for my part, do not like images cut out in juniper or other garden stuff; they be for children," and there have been many since the famous Chancellor's day who have agreed with him. Opinion is certainly sharply divided upon the question of the desirability or otherwise of adorning the garden with cut hedges and artificially shaped trees. We shall

FIG. 44.—A Sunk Formal Garden.

they possess the essence of its harmony, which, added to their suitability for assuming the conventional forms of art, make them so valuable to us. Nothing gives finer character to a garden than boundaries of massive yew hedge, nor has the brilliant colour of flowers a better foil than dwarf borders of yew or box. And so much is this true that we need never be in danger of planting in excess, for with a little skill and judgment every additional hedge or parterre will bring a measure of increased richness and beauty.

Topiary work, though unending in its possibilities, may be divided into three main divisions: the treatment of hedges, the shaping of isolated trees, and the network filling for formal gardens which ranges in size from the simple parterre to the elaborate maze or labyrinth, covering a very extended area. Of the yew hedge we have already spoken, of its arched, buttressed, recessed or battlemented forms. Loop-holes can be made through it, while cresting, finials and a thousand cut shapes can vary its skyline, their number being restricted only by the size of the hedge and the amount of labour available. And with or without these extra adornments the hedge can be massed into central or flanking towers of green with which we can vary the scenic background indefinitely.

Detached trees cut into simple pyramids, cones, cubes, or spheres, planted alone, in pairs, or in a long series, form excellent material for the designer. To mark and graduate the long terrace or walk, to emphasise the salient points of a formal enclosure or lawn, to furnish a flat, level site which would otherwise be bare and featureless, and to stand as green pillars beside a gate or archway, a seat or flight of steps,—for all these purposes they have no rival. And where some further licence is permitted, we may group our clipped yews, uniting them in single arches, open cages, cross hoops, pagodas, and terminate them with a finial of bird or beast, such as used to adorn the stone gables and oak stair-newels of the Early Stuarts. Grown out of the natural tree, these shapely forms elude the restrictions of our artificial scale, and look well whatever their size or bulk. The giant sentinels at the cottage gate do not dwarf the low whitewashed walls, nor do a full assembly of these sombre forms impair the enclosures of the largest garden.

Fig. 45.—Formal Garden, St. Alban's Court.

The labyrinth, maze, or the smaller parterres of geometric design in yew and box are a welcome variation to the enclosed flower garden. Their even appearance of quiet green rests the eye, and however eccentric the forms which the topiary artist may display in his filling, the repose is still there, for the shapes are conquered by the soft colour and yielding texture. Simple geometric patterns, scrolls, and knots, interwoven lines imitating embroidery, severely square forms or fat round shapes, lend themselves equally well to fill the borders. The fancy may let itself go in suggesting roughly the outlines of crouching bears, Indian gods, mushrooms, pots, cup and ball, and a hundred varieties of a similar nature. It is a kind of green jewellery spread upon the ground, and readily fills the space allotted to it. All topiary work requires much care and labour; but wherever it appears, whether in a single tree or in an elaborate series of gardens, it rewards the gardener with a peculiar sense of satisfaction; it is a witness to the thought and time expended upon it, it weds the garden to the human fancy, and is one of the fullest and most delightful embodiments of the idea of garden architecture.

Treillage and Ironwork

Those of our readers who are ready to appreciate the importance and charm of architectural forms in the garden, and who feel any sympathy with the principles which we have tried to set forth, will not be surprised at our advocacy of a more general use of treillage than is to be seen at the present day. The French *treillageurs* who, under Le Nôtre and

Mansart, brought this art to perfection, were only elaborating a custom which seems to have existed from the earliest days of garden-making. If we accept the principle that gardens must be laid out in orderly array, and that the outlines must be prepared which Nature herself will fill in good time, we are in need at once of an effective method of setting out the garden and indicating its future development. The light and inexpensive character of trellis-work lends itself most readily to this purpose, and its adaptability to almost any shape enables us to raise a pattern in a few days of the boundaries and features which will take years of growth and attention to mature.

From this practical use treillage has developed into an even greater importance, and has come to fill a complete department of garden design. Practically every kind of architectural structure can be imitated in trellis, and curiously enough the imitation often adapts itself to the garden scheme more perfectly than the original itself. A garden enclosed by a trellis screen, with arches, pilasters, arbours, etc., of the same material, may be made a place of great delight, but it will depend very much

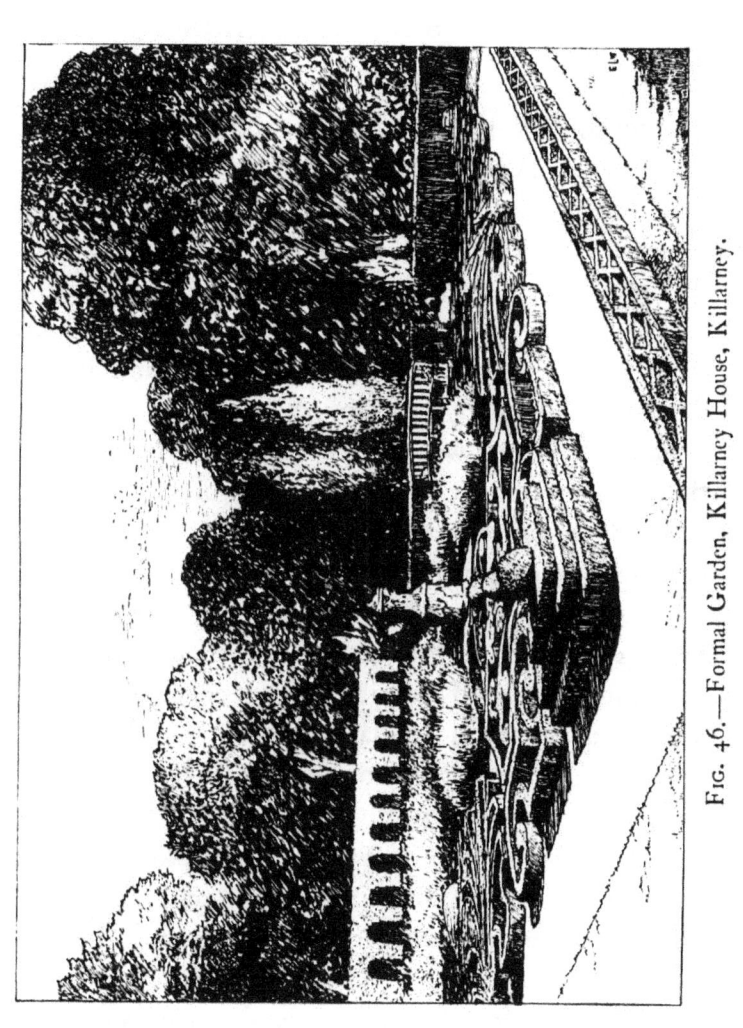

Fig. 46.—Formal Garden, Killarney House, Killarney.

on the forms employed: the idea must be well conceived, and the detail must be worthy of the conception. Trellis may easily become commonplace or tawdry, and unless it is to be entirely covered with foliage its structural lines should give the appearance, as well as have the reality, of strength.

There are many places in the garden where treillage can be effectively introduced, and it can generally be safely employed wherever our immediate forebears would have been tempted to use the so-called "rustic" type of woodwork. Temples, arbours, summer houses, screens, enclosures for tennis lawns or paved gardens, the backs of seats, all these are easily formed of this material. Although, however, it is a useful method to employ here and there, it is better, if possible, to make such features a definite part of a treillage scheme, and to link a seat or shelter to a screen of trellis, self-supporting or fixed to the face of a wall. Treillage gives a definite character to the garden in which it is employed, and it is invaluable on new sites and in town gardens, where well-grown hedges and trees are absent. Yet its beauty is greatly enhanced by a background of trees, which can be seen through its semi-transparent wall.

TREILLAGE AND IRONWORK

Where expense is no object, a garden adorned with treillage architecture is a most desirable addition to the grounds, and provides a beautiful and quite harmonious variation to the other enclosures. The woodwork can be varied, too, by wrought iron, after the delightful models of the eighteenth century, though the outlay is, of course, much increased, and the painting and repair of the smith's craftsmanship form a serious part of the general upkeep.

Fig. 47.—Garden House of Treillage.

X

WATER, STONE, AND LEAD

Pools and Fountains

THE picture of the garden domain is certainly not complete without the grateful presence of the pool or fountain. The three elements of water, earth, and sky, when the sun is at its height, form a unity which is sadly broken when the first-named is lacking. Not that water is essential to the garden, for where the site does not provide a stream it is often a difficult and costly matter to introduce it. Yet it is worth having whenever possible, for the sake of the companionship between it and the flowers, and of the cool freshness which pervades the atmosphere wherever the still surface of the pool or the restless movement of the fountain is to be seen.

Where a stream runs through the garden, or is

near enough to provide a rivulet which can be conducted through the grounds, we can make use of it in various ways. If there is an appreciable fall in the ground we can scheme a cascade both at its entrance and its departure from the garden, leading the water in a single spout to fall into a circular pool. Where the volume of water is small, a little stone-edged canal may be formed along the centre or the side of a lawn or flower garden, enlarging itself into square or circular pools at various points, and left clear or planted with flag and rush at pleasure. The narrow, straight line of water between its stone margins is a pretty feature in a formal garden, and is a simple method of conducting the water towards and away from a central pool.

Where the stream is of larger dimensions, it will be well to treat it architecturally for some part of its length at least. The natural winding bank of a river is, of course, delightful in its passage through meadowland or wooded glades, but in the garden the straight margin is the more appropriate, and has in it greater possibilities of beauty. The various types of wall and balustrading described in our earlier pages for terraces will make an excellent boundary along the bank and will be reflected pleasantly below, giving, moreover, convenient points for bridging the stream. Bridges show in common with other features of garden architecture the necessity for some regularity of form to ensure success, the absence of which sufficiently accounts for the failure of the "rustic" types. In large gardens the roofed "Palladian" bridge of stone provides the opportunity for the most dignified compositions, and even in smaller sites a roofed bridge of timber (connected, perhaps, with a garden house or water pavilion) combines an orthodox treatment with real picturesqueness. The bridges in figs. 49 and 50 show two simple designs, the one a wooden bridge with stone abutments, the other—wholly of stone—built in the mediæval manner.

Of pools and fountains there are an enormous number of historical and modern examples from which to choose. The fish-pond near the house is, in itself, a thing of beauty, as at Brickwall, Northiam (fig. 48), but it monopolises a good deal of space. The more favourite form of pool is either the brimful type edged with a simple stone margin

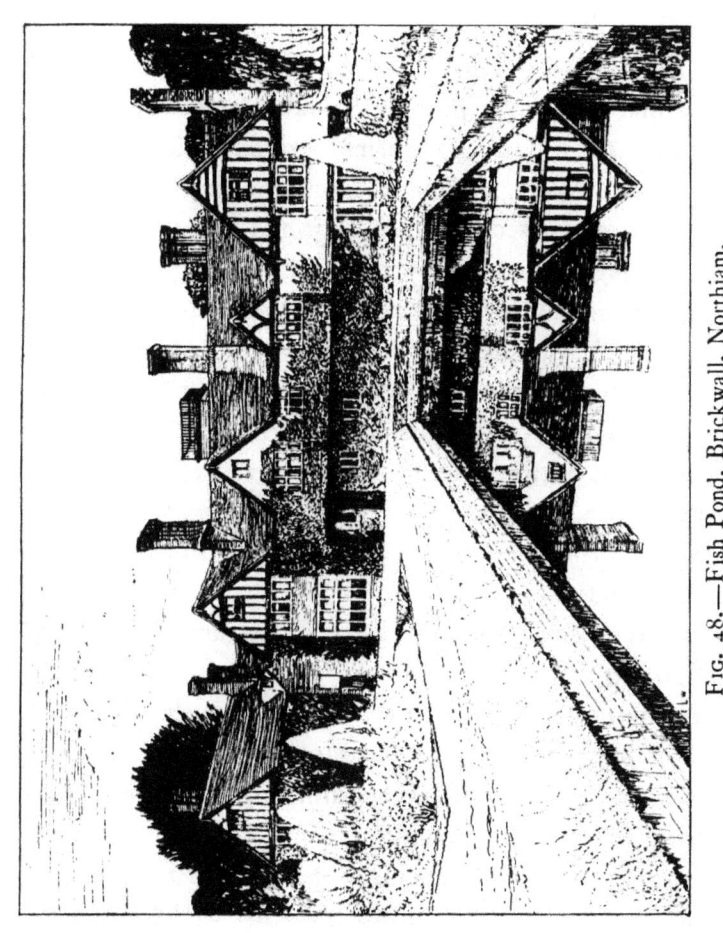

Fig. 48.—Fish Pond, Brickwall, Northiam.

level with the ground, or the balustraded form which is protected by stone balusters following its outline. The former is equally suitable to the centre of a lawn, a formal paved court, or an enclosed flower garden. The pool in the formal enclosure at Ascott House (fig. 30) is of this type, and it is surrounded by turf, immediately adjoining the stone. A level stretch of stone paving or turf is, indeed, the ideal setting for water, variety being introduced by the size and shape of the surface. A great number of designs can be made, all of simple geometric outline—long, square, circular, elliptical—with the addition of a few re-entering angles, scrolls, twists, or curves that serve to give them interest and variation.

Garden fountains are usually best arranged when spouting from the centre of a pool, though there are naturally many positions where the isolated basin supported by an architectural or sculptured base will be desired. Unending ingenuity has been expended in the invention of wondrous fountains and cascades for the princely gardens of the Renaissance, and there is infinite pleasure to be obtained from fine combinations of sculpture and spraying

Fig. 49.—A Stone Bridge.

endow those garden enclosures wherein he weds nature to art. The sculptured vase, the urn, the figure in lead or stone,—each is beautiful in its contrast with the foliage and bloom of the garden, and yet it has a secret kinship and sympathy with its surroundings. It is a symbol, a sign of man's interest in nature as a whole, and an indication of his appreciation of the fact that the unity in the isolated work of art is a reflection, however imperfect, of the greater unity in Universal Nature herself. This at least is the mood in which we contemplate these silent inhabitants of the garden, and for this reason we hold that they should be as perfect in water. The simple jet, however, can be used with remarkable effect in many positions in the garden. It brings life and gaiety wherever it appears, whether flung from the centre or sides of a pool, or from amidst a mass of flowers, or issuing perhaps from a lonely wall, where it makes a gentle music ever ready to surprise and gladden the ear.

Figures and Vases of Stone and Lead

Garden figures, vases, and the like, appear to some people as merely the stage properties of the outdoor scenic artist, and the same prejudice attaches to them that we have noted in the case of all architecturally guided design. It is true, of course, that many examples of these ornaments, both on account of their poor quality and ill-devised position, are deserving of censure; but it is no less true that, properly disposed, they are inhabitants of the garden domain as welcome as the very trees and flowers themselves. They represent one of the many ways of introducing the human element,—the product of fancy, of the poetic imagination, and of the love of symmetry and graceful outline, with which it is man's part to

FIGURES AND VASES OF STONE AND LEAD 179

Fig. 50.—A Stone and Timber Bridge.

form and as exquisite in workmanship as possible, always remembering that the material must be such as lends itself to the softening influence of time. Marble and terra-cotta should, as a rule, be avoided, since the former loses its first beauty, and the latter resists all the efforts of the weather to tone its harshness. But freestone and lead are materials which are capable of the most delightful modelling, while both submit themselves to the increasing charm of age.

The vase and urn, unless of unusual size, are commonly an accessory to some more important feature. They tend to be mean and superfluous if placed along the margin of a lawn or walk, but in conjunction with a balustrade, a flight of steps, or a low retaining wall they may be of great value. In paved enclosures or on a flagged terrace they are especially appropriate, and seem to be the natural growths of the level stone floor; it is for this reason that they are often the staple part of the design for town or roof gardens. But they are also of great charm when in close proximity to masses of foliage or even to the untamed growth of climbing roses and similar plants. Thus they are beautiful finials to gate piers, isolated pedestals, boundary walls, and in many situations of a somewhat deserted nature they are ready to recall to us our own human ideals and to give a sense of comfort and companionship.

The whole class of architectural ornaments, which includes vases, urns, and various forms of the sculptor's art, lies ready to hand when we wish to provide a central feature, to give some emphasis to certain points and situations in the design, or again to add some subtle element of beauty which will not easily come otherwise. Sculpture *per se*, that is to say, the figure—alone or grouped—is an expensive matter, and it pertains to a high and rare form of art which does not admit of anything second rate. There are, however, certain figures which are tolerable, even when not the work of an undisputed master,—subjects which are perfectly adapted to the garden and equally attractive when carved in stone or cast in lead. Among these, the most charming are figures of children,—whether impersonating Cupid or exhibiting any other particular quality, good or reprehensible, it is no matter. In a courtyard or amid the flowers, on a gate pier, in a niche of yew or brick, or emerging from the waters of a pool, the naked child is always a fresh and vigorous figure. Peasant children in their costume are not inappropriate,—they look at home in the garden,—but the easiest selection will be made from the animal world, from which every situation can be supplied with something interesting and fitting. It is not, however, every artist who can best serve the requirements of the garden in this matter of sculpture. The modelling should be robust and full, for the outline will have an exaggerated importance seen against the sky or a background of green. Garden sculpture

Fig. 51.—A Wall Fountain.

has its own qualities, and very charming they are when the artist catches the right spirit and produces something in conformity therewith.

Boxes and Tubs for Trees and Flowers

The artificial receptacle for the growth of plant, tree, or flower takes a leading part in the equipment of the garden. The common garden pot is the most essential part of the whole practical machinery of gardening, and when we would put the pot and its occupant in some special place in our design, we should exchange it for a somewhat bigger, more adaptable, and more presentable form. There are many things which can be made to hold enough soil for this purpose: vases and urns, other than those designed for pure ornament, wooden circular tubs, square framed boxes, well-heads, and lead cisterns. The last named are well adapted to a position in the centre of a pool or stream (fig. 30), from which the flowers can hang to the water's surface. Tubs can be built up of brick or stonework, and a succession of these elevated beds will make an appropriate change in certain situations.

All boxes, tubs, and urns which are to hold plants or dwarf trees should be of ample size, and be either set upon the ground or upon a good structural base. Nothing of a small or flimsy nature should be admitted—for it is neither practical nor comely. As in our flower borders it should be our aim to provide the means for the most luxuriant growth, so nothing but a mass of colour or a finely shaped head of green should give the excuse for the presence of these similar but isolated features.

The box and tub pertain to courtyards, to paved terraces and walks. They may at times take the place of the mere ornament on a stairway (fig. 34), or each side of a seat. But their most obvious duty is to bring colour or greenery into those places where the paved surface precludes planting, and to bring it in a manner which fits with its formal character. Hence their value in town or roof gardens, and in courtyards surrounded by buildings. When filled with flowers, they can easily and quickly be replanted, or when furnished with choice trees they can be brought out or removed into shelter at will. The monotony—if it exist—of a paved terrace along the whole front of a brick or stone

Fig. 52.—Pool in an Enclosed Garden.

house is never so effectively dispelled as by a row of orange trees, or plants of clipped box, etc., which, ranged against the wall, complete a most desirable picture. In the same way any amount of colour can be introduced on a terrace or along a walk. The tub or box is a movable flower bed, and has all the possibilities which its mobility gives it. And because it is in itself a unit which can be multiplied indefinitely, it is one of the most useful factors in the formal garden. Placed at the angles of the geometrical designs, emphasising the salient points, relieving the squares of paving, it has the merit of raising the flowers and foliage to a higher level, and thus introduces an important feature into the design. Alone, in series, or in quantity, it is an instrument which cannot be disregarded, but used with care and tastefully filled it will bring to the garden an amazing amount of joy and gaiety.

Sundials

The sundial, the most popular of garden ornaments, is in danger of becoming too frequent a feature, and of losing its own poetic character in a display of affectation of which it is sometimes the sign. We are well aware that to a number of people, yet unconvinced that "landscape" gardening is not the most fitting method of laying out our grounds, the whole teaching of formal gardening appears a transient pose and mere affectation. We have, however, tried to show that this teaching rests on sure foundations, and that architectural principles and garden design must go together if we are to get results at all befitting the beauty and importance of the subject. It is therefore our aim, while encouraging the fullest expression of the artist's invention and fancy, —as long as it yields to the discipline of the simple rules of the art,---to avoid the inclusion of features

Fig. 53.—Enclosed Garden and Sundial.

or designs which are clearly anachronisms, and of objects which have not a real value in the garden scheme.

But the sundial in its essence is a very practical affair. It is a dial to tell us the hour of the day, though as such it has long been superseded by the clock and watch. In earlier days, sundials were put up wherever people met together, in the market place, on the village green, or on the church wall. Moreover, as with all useful things in the days when art was a common possession, it was invested with a simple beauty, and to people whose souls were full of symbolism its mission had a genuine appeal until it seemed to personify the spirit of time. So it comes about that we, who live in a materialistic age, are apt to find the sundial, with its old associations, a more poetic instrument than the clocks and chronometers of the present day, though perhaps the latter are more entitled to our contemplative thoughts than the imperfect dial of the past.

Still there is this to be urged in favour of the continued use of the sundial—its construction and material are both eminently fitted to its place out of doors, and it makes use of the natural movements of sunshine and shadow which are part and parcel of the garden and all that grows therein. If, therefore, we decide to include the sundial in our gardens, let us see to it that it does its work, that it is set in the sunlight, and that its dial is properly calculated for its position.

The pedestal dial is the most attractive form, and the simple or enriched baluster the best pattern, when placed on a lawn or in the centre of a formal enclosure for flowers (figs. 24 and 53). A plain stone platform level with the turf is enough to rest it upon, and it should seldom be made to look pretentious. But there are other dials which should not be neglected. The sundial on the wall or on the vertical face of a tall pillar was more common than the pedestal dial in days gone by. The pillar is a beautiful feature amid the flowers, for it can be raised to a good height and lends itself to charming design. The wall dial, too, has a wonderfully decorative value, and on the sides of the house, of a garden shelter, or of a gate pier, it gives that added touch of interest which is often so valuable. Lastly, the dial with figures of box or yew planted in a wide circle on the turf is a feature which will bear repetition, and is worthy of a more frequent inclusion in the topiary work of modern gardens.

XI

SOME SPECIAL GARDENS

The Kitchen Garden

THE kitchen garden is the one enclosure which has retained a large part of its ancient formality, in spite of opposite tendencies in the recent fashions of flower borders and lawns. Here, where utility bears undisputed sway, the old-time beauty has sheltered under her wing, and has laughed securely since no one thought the homely and serviceable lines of the kitchen garden were worthy of the attentions of the landscape gardener. Thus we have come to know, and feel an affection for, the high walls round a plot four square, the long straight paths dividing up the area into rectangular divisions, and the borders of flowers, the intrusion of which is never forbidden or regretted.

The contrast, then, which of late existed between

the kitchen garden and the remainder of our pleasance will, we hope, disappear, and with the return of the main gardens to the older methods, there will be a harmony between the useful and charming qualities of both. Our only aim will be to preserve and confirm the simple lines which were set out so many years ago.

The kitchen garden requires shelter first and foremost, and this can be satisfactorily obtained only by high walls. This initial outlay must be met, and although, in small gardens, hedges and fences may often be made to serve, they cannot vie with the solid wall in efficiency or in general usefulness. The wall, unlike the hedge, takes no nourishment from the ground, and it will yield a fine harvest of fruit from the trees trained up its sides. Proper economy of space in vegetable and fruit growing requires method and a formal arrangement in straight lines; for this reason the enclosure should be rectangular, its walls should have few openings in them, and the general character of the boundaries should be as restful and solid as possible. The walls, of a height from seven to twelve feet, should have a projecting coping to throw the rain clear of the fruit trees, and the effect will be improved if outbuildings and other structures outside the boundary but linked with it be utilised for additional shelter and for varying the skyline of the enclosure. With good gates, preferably of wrought iron, between tall piers or hung beneath an archway, and with any of the pleasant variations in the character of the walling or in the direction of its outline, the whole framework of the garden can be made extraordinarily attractive and picturesque.

The plot itself, if of ordinary size, can be divided into four squares by two central paths crossing one another at right angles, and another path can be carried round the garden separating the beds beneath the walls from the main area. Along the two intersecting central paths there can be a border of gaily-coloured old-fashioned flowers, making a brilliant cross, the arms of which reach from the centre almost to the boundary. And in the middle an open tank of water, with curb of brick, stone, or lead, is the most fitting feature wherein, moreover, some little adornment may be indulged, some enrichment of modelling or even a lead figure. And as to the paths, stone or brick paving is the best; but gravel,

Fig. 54.—Wall of Kitchen Garden, Dalingridge Place.

sand, or ashes can be used. If these are many, the byways can be turfed, thus adding greatly to the garden's beauty, but the main walks should be of a material hard enough to bear the traffic of barrow or trolley.

Of fruit trees, the larger sort should be assembled in their own orchards, or as single trees they may be placed in the most favourable positions, and not necessarily in the kitchen garden itself. We have already spoken of the arcaded walk and pergola of fruit trees; they are never out of place in the flower and pleasure gardens, for at all times they are objects of beauty. The smaller sort, however, espaliers, canes, and bushes, are best kept together, and need an effective protection from birds. This can best be obtained, and in a manner quite consonant with the formal design, by wire netting raised on a square framework which will enclose and roof in one end of the garden. Thus, within methodical and regular lines the kitchen garden will furnish a show of natural wealth and unrivalled charm, and will tempt us to walk within its borders with the same pleasure which we feel among the other parts of our garden territory.

The Town and Roof Garden

The problem which the town garden presents is one of a very particular kind. It is circumscribed in space, and it is limited by the difficulty of rearing many trees and plants which languish in an atmosphere of streets and houses. From the latter consideration a greater importance attaches to the architectural plan and to the structural features of the garden, and moreover, it suggests the propriety of planting out and placing flowers which have been reared elsewhere in tubs, urns, and raised beds where they can flower and be replaced by others from the same source. The limitation of space practically imposes upon us a severe formality of plan, with an added care in respect of a design which stands alone and permanently before us, and is easily scrutinised in all its detail.

But the conditions of the town garden plan, however difficult they may be, are in fact the source of its unique beauty. There is no plot, small though it be, which cannot be made into the most enticing miniature paradise ; and although, of course, a certain amount of expenditure is entailed, it need never be as great as in a larger area, and no part of the effect is lost. The first thing to remember is that the important view of the garden is from the house,— this is the permanent view, observed at all times, and it should be set as a scene in a theatre, the house occupying the position of the auditorium. The problem is that of the formal garden, viewed chiefly from one end. It is also conditioned by the main principles, discussed in our earlier pages, which should guide the relationship of garden and house.

The plan in fig. 55 shows a small town house

with a garden some 115 feet long by 60 feet wide. The house was to one side of the plot, and by a happy chance a fine hawthorn, about a third of the length of the garden from the house, was in line with the outer wall and divided the width into two parts—one of the same dimension as the building, and the other coinciding with the distance of the house from the boundary wall. This suggested and facilitated the division of the area, lengthways, into a wider portion on an axial line with the house and a narrow strip suitable for a side walk. A reference to the design will show how the former or main portion was treated. The chief floor being several feet above the ground level, a stone terrace was planned with a double flight of steps merging into one flight below. This led into a small flagged garden with shaped beds, bounded by a stone balustrade. In these beds any amount of colour could be introduced, and the balustrading divided this, the foreground of the picture, from the larger portion beyond. The main area was laid out with a geometric pattern of narrow stone paths across turf, with a small pond in the centre. A border for flowers or shrubs with scolloped edges

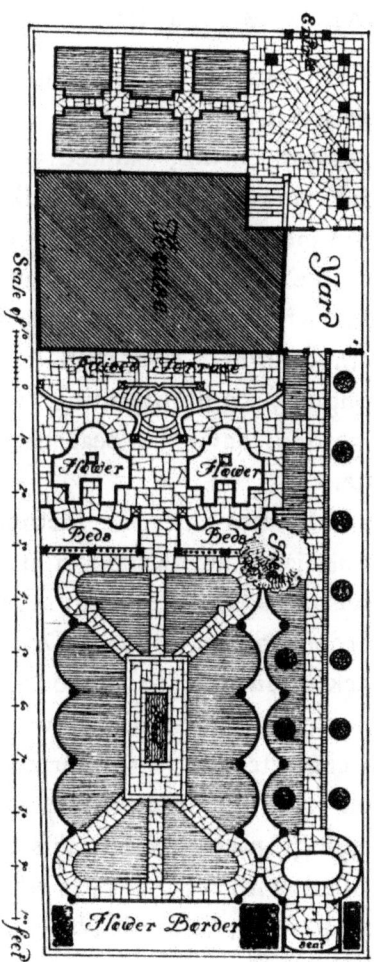

Fig. 55.—A Town Garden.

was carried along each side, the points of the curves being emphasised by cut trees in boxes. At the end a wide flower border, banked up to the wall, completed the view. The long walk, also paved, was marked on either side by a series of cut bushes, set, towards the garden, in the curves of the scolloped beds which were repeated to correspond with the main design. The path terminated with an elliptical figure, communicating with the lower end of the garden, having a seat between yews to close the vista.

This plan illustrates but one method of treating a small rectangular plan, although it indicates the value of a division of the area into separate portions when the garden admits of it. One of the most successful backgrounds is to be found in a garden house, designed with a certain amount of definite architectural character and supported by an extension either side in brick or stonework. The whole intervening space between this and the house can then be filled with formal beds edged with box, or by turf and paving; and tubs, boxes, and urns for flowers can be put at various points to graduate the distance. We may perhaps refer in this connection to a beautiful little garden designed by Mr. E. L. Lutyens for Sir Hugh Lane at Chelsea, where an overhanging tree is reflected in a circular pool in the centre of a lawn which is intersected by paved walks. The two side paths terminate each in a beautiful little architectural composition in brick, having niches for figures, these being the main features in the composition.

The town garden requires furnishing to a much greater degree than the grounds of a country house. The setting, too, is all-important, and a pleasant architectural treatment of the surrounding walls, with appropriate recesses, summer houses, alcoves, or standing-places for figures in lead and stone, will solve the whole problem, leaving the central area to be paved or turfed in a simple way and brightened by some beautiful flowers set in receptacles prepared for them. A comparatively inexpensive method of obtaining the same effect is to surround the garden with well-designed treillage, which, if carried to a proper height and relieved by some interesting features, will provide the required shelter and set the fitting scenery for the little stage. The analogy of the theatre suggests itself most readily, but it is not to be thought that the aim is towards anything implied in the term "theatrical." The position of the site in the town requires an architectural setting, but the effect should be quiet, orderly, and dignified, with as much interest as is compatible with these qualities.

Roof gardens should be controlled by similar principles, but on a smaller scale. Treillage and ironwork form the best boundaries, and a simple form of paving the most appropriate field. Into these box beds, tubs, vases, and urns can be introduced for flowers, and at various points arches or cages can be erected for climbing plants. Seats are the more necessary where space for walking is limited, and their arrangement will depend on whether there is a view to look upon, or whether they are to be set to avoid an unpleasant prospect and to concentrate the attention on the garden itself.

Rock Gardens

We close this brief *résumé* of the principles of garden planning with a few lines on what has been to too many a stumbling-block in their progress towards a rational plan. The delight of the creeping plant and the thousand species of alpine and other close-growing and gaily-coloured flowers, has led almost every type of gardener to strew some part of his ground with formless *débris* and trust to its being covered in time with the glory of the flowers. The "grotto" of the late eighteenth century became the "rockery" of the nineteenth, and we have not yet grown out of this pertinacious habit which creeps in at inopportune moments and ruins an otherwise good scheme.

First, then, we would suggest that a rock garden is so beautiful a thing that it is worth doing well. It should take its place as one of the definite divisions of the garden, and should have a worthy approach and a fitting setting. Second, let the stones of which it is to be composed resemble in some degree the natural stratification of the quarry, for Nature seldom tosses her material in a confused heap, save in her angry and volcanic moods. And third, there is no reason why the rock garden should not possess a certain regularity of lay-out, and conform to the general principles of our plan. The flowers themselves require no restraint, they will multiply, and throw a riot of colour over the banks of stone, whether these latter follow a coherent design or are placed in merely irregular array. The mass of colour is indeed more often effective when it surrounds a sunk garden of a roughly symmetrical shape than when it is broken up into disordered parts. The habit of mind which connects the rock garden with a pile of stones, is apt to regard it as a feature applicable to any position where it seems to get over a difficulty or an odd corner. Let us regard the rock garden seriously, and honour it by giving it, as well as all other things in the garden, a proper place, and let us face the difficulties of each part of our plan courageously until we find the right solution. *Est* locus *in rebus* should be our motto, or as it might be written for us—*est* locus *in hortis*; and if we make this our guiding principle, we shall find our plan coherent and our garden truly beautiful.

Fig. 58

Plan of Ashdown Place, Forest Row

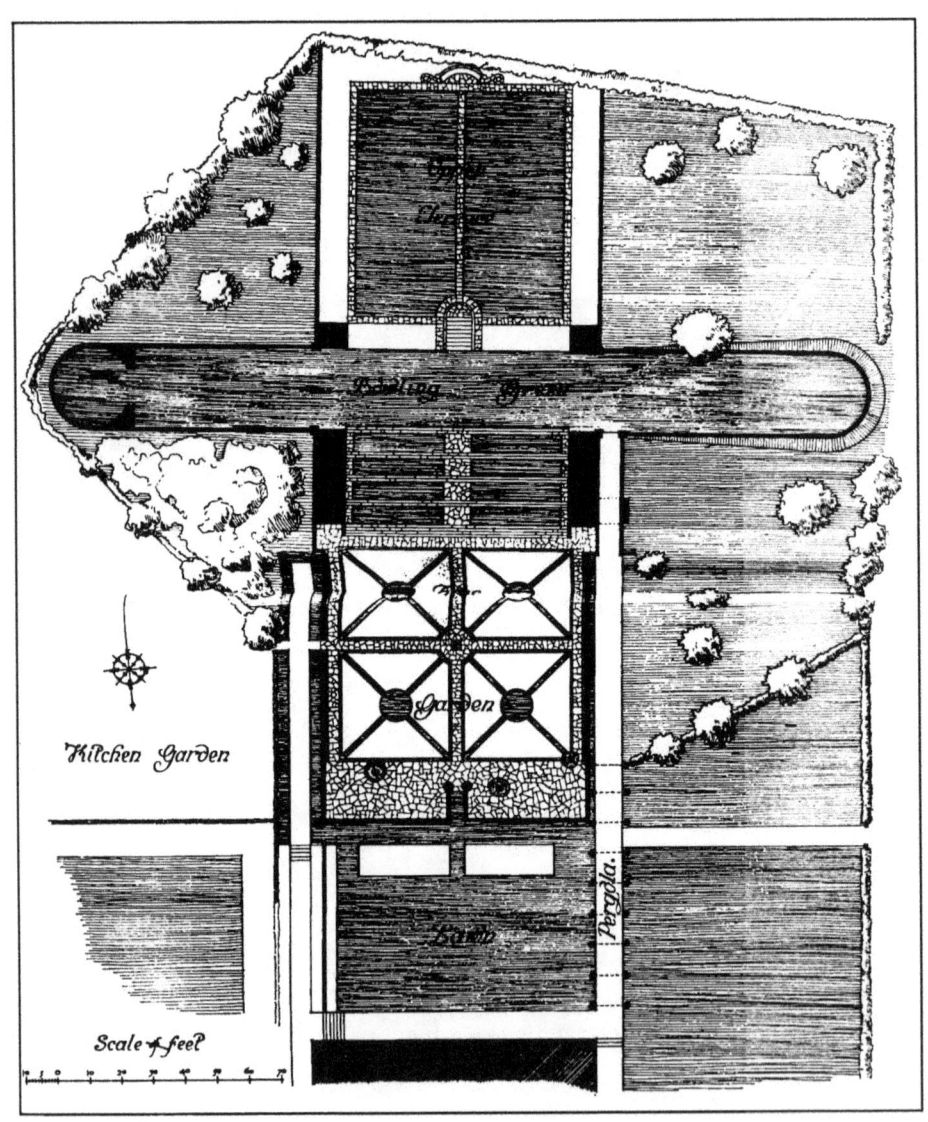

Fig. 58.—Plan of Ashdown Place, Forest Row.

Fig. 59

Design for Stansted Park

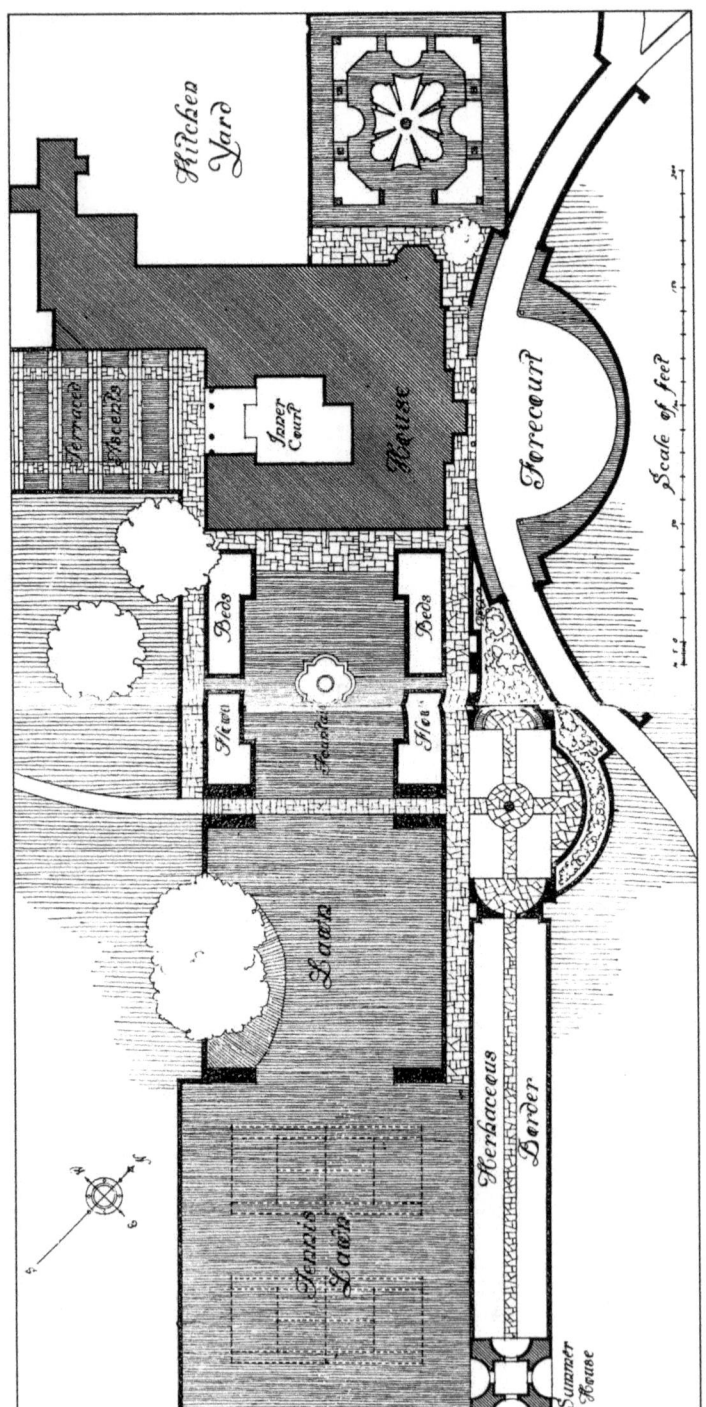

Fig. 59.—Designer Stansted Park.

Fig. 60

Plan of Coombe Warren, Kingston Hill

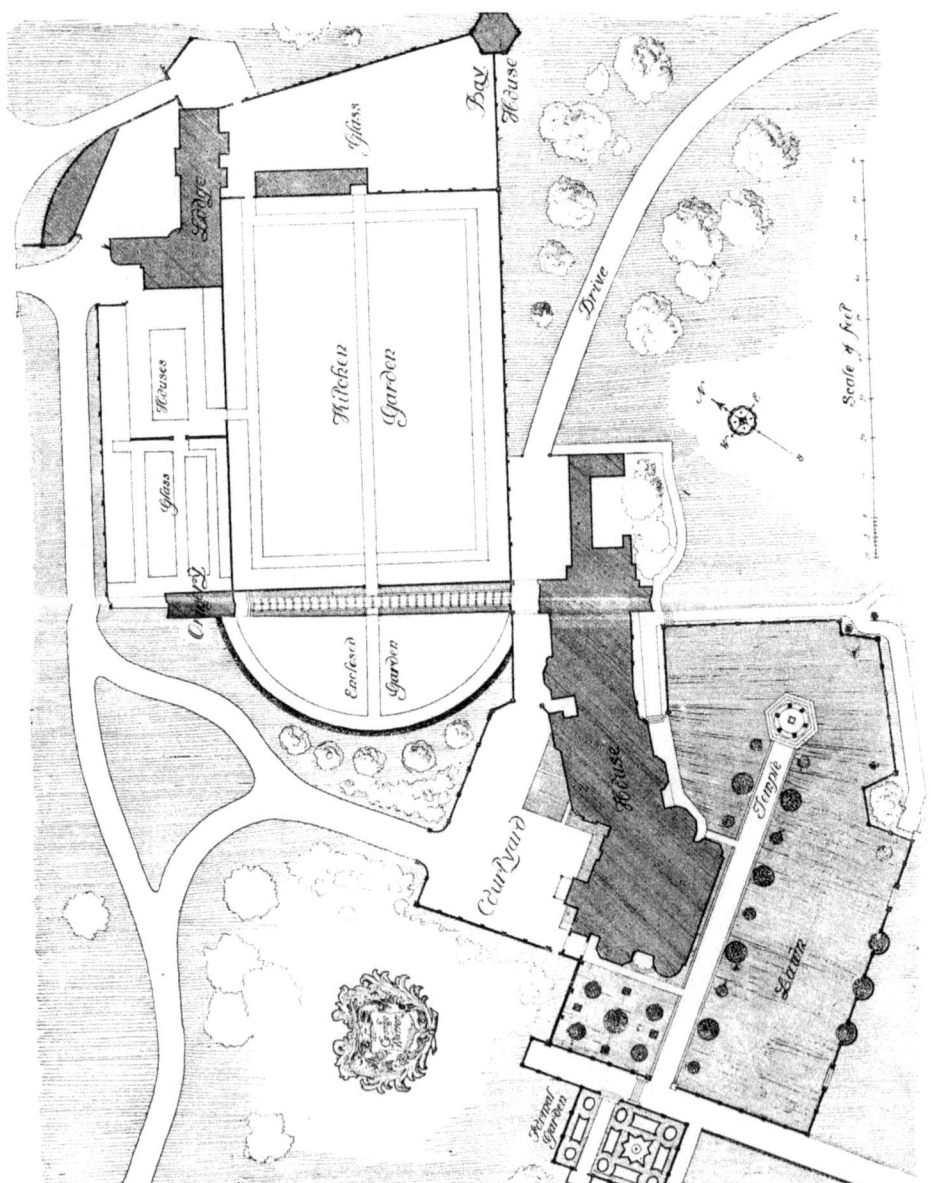

Fig. 60.—Plan of Coomb Warren, Kingston Hill.

Fig. 61

Plan of Henley Hall, Ludlow

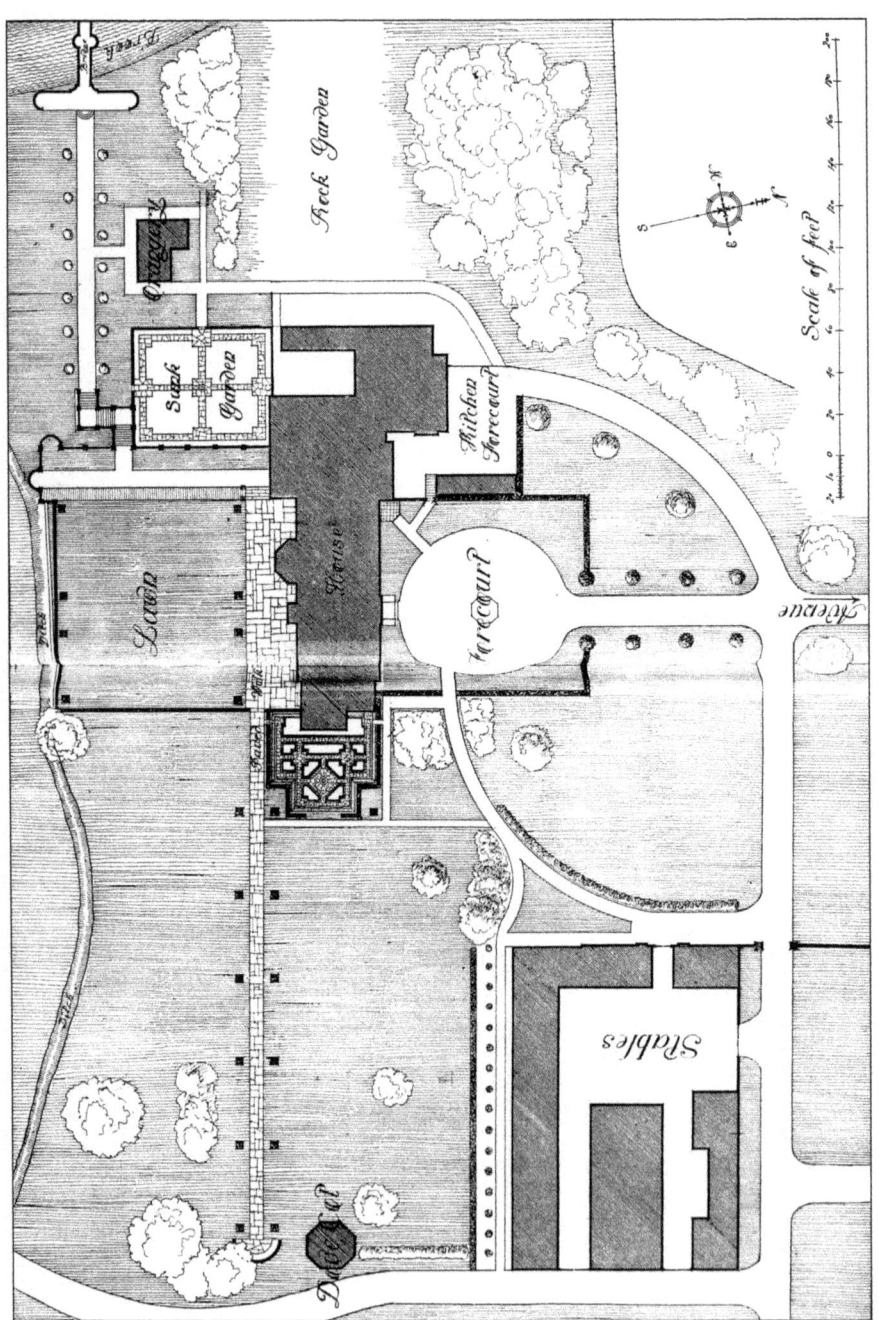

Fig. 61.—Plan of Henley Hall, Ludlow.

Fig. 62

A Typical Plan for a Small Garden

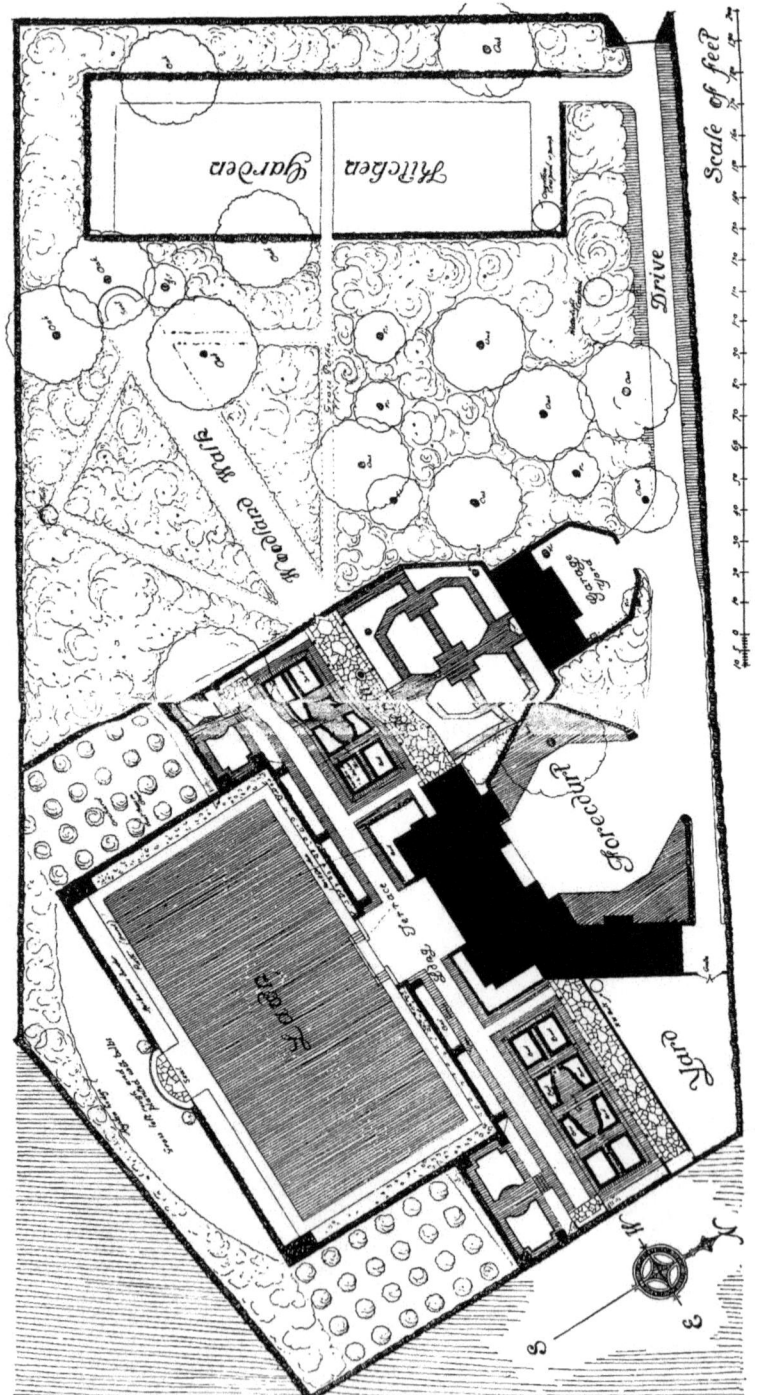

Fig. 62.—A Typical Plan for a Small Garden.

Fig. 63

Plan showing an Arrangement for Planting

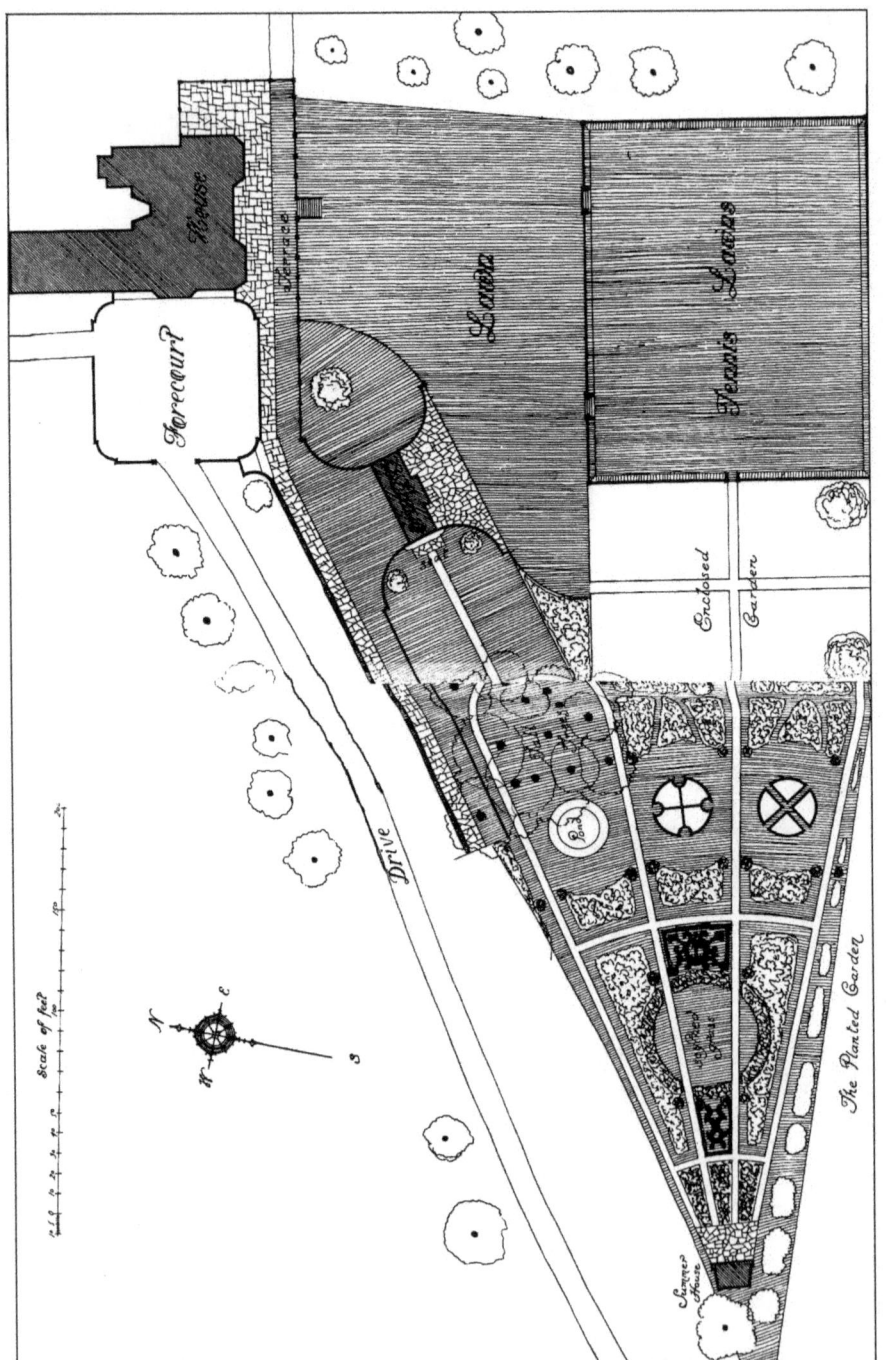

Fig. 63.—Plan showing an arrangement for Planting.

Fig. 56

Plan of Elm-Tree Farm, West Wittering

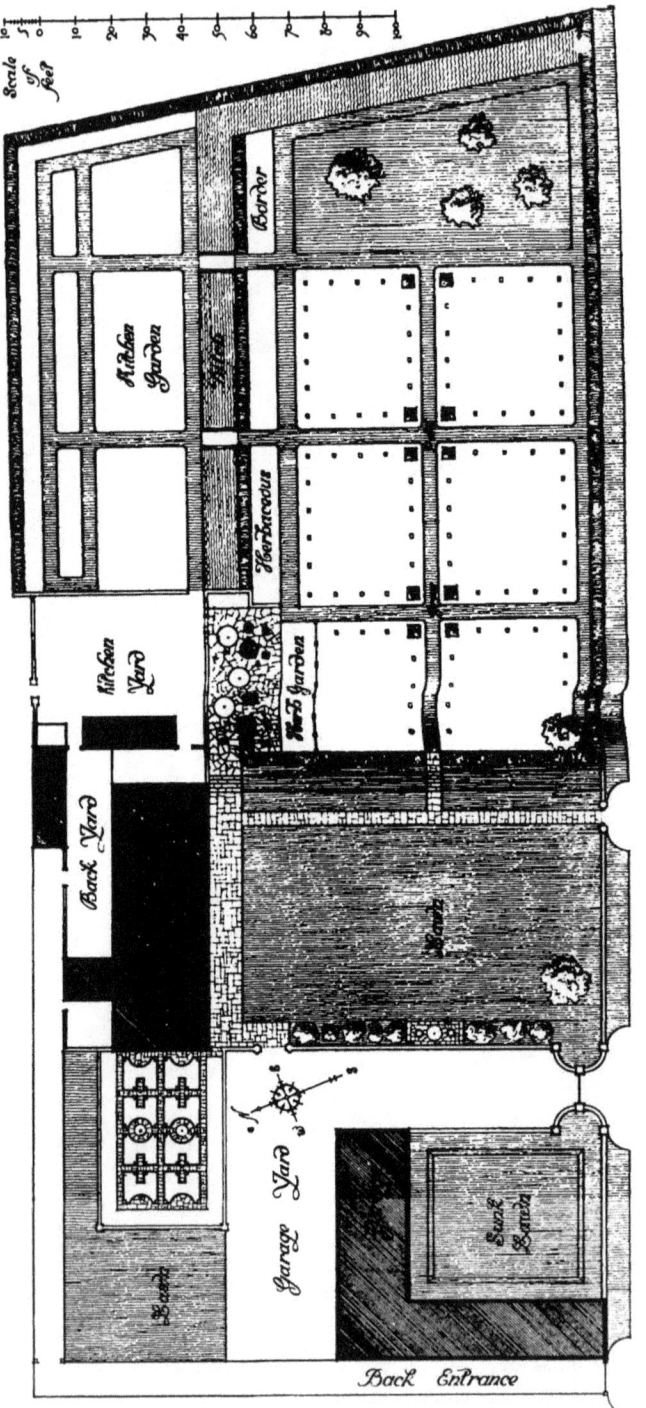

Fig. 56.—Plan of Elm-Tree Farm, West Wittering.

Fig. 57

Plan of Dalingridge Place, West Hoathly

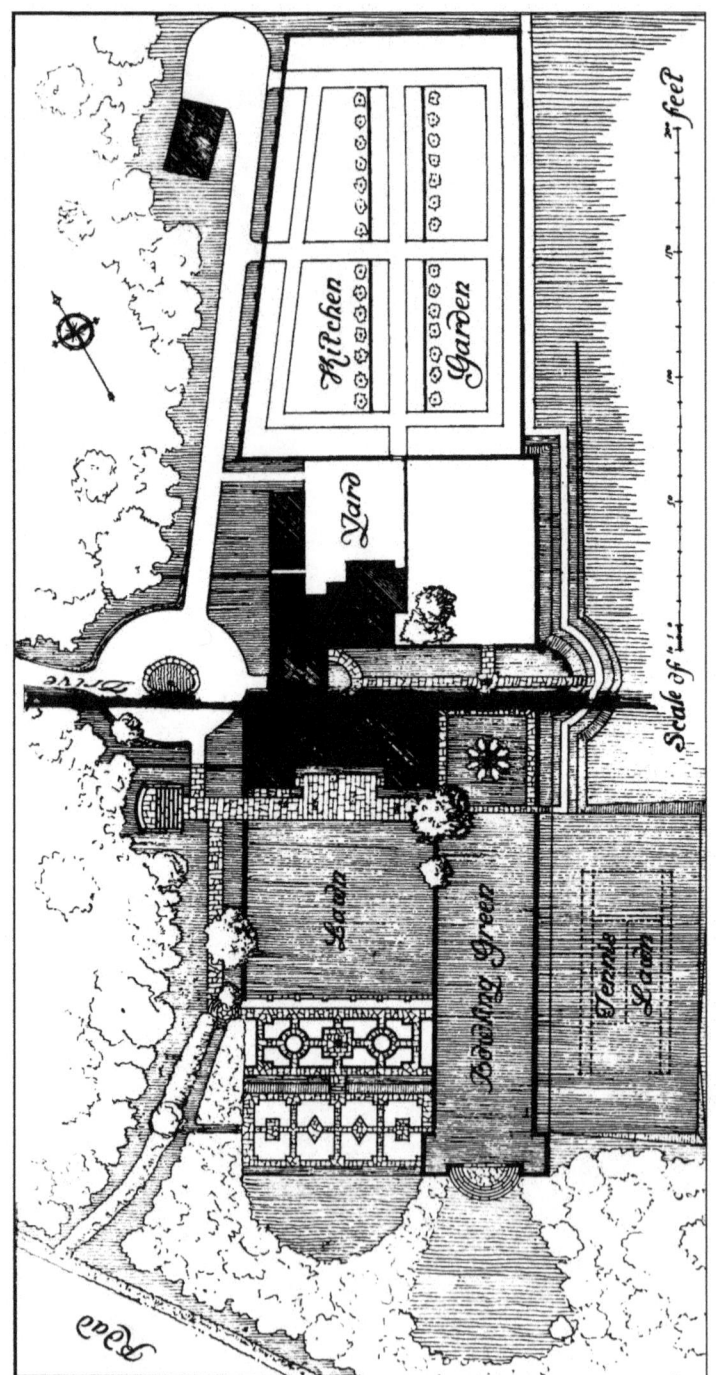

Fig. 57.—Plan of Dalingridge Place, West Hoathly.

INDEX

A

Alterations to old houses, 32-35
Appledram, Tower House, 43
Arbours, 9, 73, 143, 144, 147, 163
Arcaded walks, 160, 161
Architects and garden design, 1, 4, 5, 7, 148
Ascott House, 9, 45, 73, 106, 115, 143, 146, 151, 176
Ashdown Place, 48, 99, 127, 133, 134, 142
Aspect of house, 29, 30, 61
Avenues, 58-60, 103

B

Balustrading, 120, 124, 125, 126, 132, 138, 176
Banks of turf, 67, 99
Bowling greens, 98, 99, 133
Box-edging, 105, 164, 189
Boxes and tubs for flowers, 69, 152, 154, 183-186, 198, 200
Brickwall, Northiam, 175
Bridges, 174, 178, 179
Building materials, 17, 72, 74, 77, 78, 135, 136, 159

C

Coombe Warren, Kingston Hill, 15, 32, 45, 92, 155

Coping for walls, 79-82
Cottage garden, the, 36, 165
Courtyards, 60-70
Courtyards enclosed on three sides, 70

D

Dalingridge Place, 35, 39, 41, 45, 49, 99, 108, 116, 120, 123, 127, 135, 136, 142, 193
Drive, the, 30, 57-60

E

Entrance courtyard, 21, 32, 61-67
Entrance gates, 50-57
Entrance to house, 20, 50-70

F

Flower enclosures, 99-108. *See* Formal Gardens
Flowers, position of, 17, 42, 44, 63, 101-104, 107, 108, 183-186, 192
Foreign features, 24
Formal gardens, 18, 44-47, 96, 97, 99-108, 109, 112, 115, 163, 166, 167, 169, 185, 195, 197
Formality in garden plans, 4, 5, 19, 47, 59
Fountains, 174, 176, 177, 182, 185

INDEX

G

Garden design, an art, 2, 61
Garden design, principles of, 8, 11, 12-28
Garden houses, 9, 26, 73, 121, 146-153, 171
Gardeners, 2
Gate piers, 89, 90
Gates, 76, 80, 86-93, 193
Gateways, 15, 18, 23, 50-57, 62, 86-93
Greenhouses, 153, 154

H

Hedges, 83-86, 105, 107, 164
Henley Hall, 32, 41, 45, 46, 112
Herbaceous borders, 44
House as background to garden, 25-28, 148
House and garden, unity between, 13, 24-28

I

Ironwork, 51, 52, 66, 80, 87, 88, 91, 92, 93, 171

K

Killarney House, Killarney, 3, 85, 99, 100, 105, 169
Kitchen garden, the, 36, 90, 96, 190-194

L

Lawns, 3, 42, 94-99
Lead figures, etc., 179, 181, 183, 199
Little Lodge, Newick, 33, 34, 40, 60, 64
Lodges, 55-57
Loggias and verandahs, 146

M

Maze and labyrinth, 164

N

Nature, her ready reponsse to guidance, 4, 8

O

Orangeries, 15, 114, 154, 155

P

Paths, 16, 22, 42, 95, 96
Paving, 15, 37, 40, 96, 106, 109-117, 126, 196, 197
Penshurst, 89, 108
Pergolas, 38, 44, 156-161
Pitchford Hall, Shrewsbury, 6, 32, 140, 146
Plaish Hall, 31, 41, 45
Plan, the garden, 29-49
Planting, 14, 16, 59, 60
Pools. *See* Water

R

Rock gardens, 200-202
Rockeries, to be avoided, 67, 75, 201
Roof gardens, 200
Rose gardens, 123. *See* Formal Gardens

S

St. Alban's Court, 105, 166
Scale in gardens, 10
Screens, wrought-iron, 92, 93
Seats, 9, 73, 139-146, 147
Stairways. *See* Steps
Stansted Park, 32
Statuary, 177, 180, 181, 199
Steps, 6, 48, 128-138
Stone paving, joints of, 111, 113, 117
Summer houses. *See* Garden houses
Sundials, 97, 186-189
Sunk gardens, 104, 105, 163

INDEX

T

Tennis lawns, 3, 98
Terrace, the principal, 21, 22, 37-41, 119-121
Terrace, the projecting, 48, 127
Terraced garden, 122
Terraces, 9, 48, 73, 118-127, 130, 141, 142, 148, 150
Tile paving, 110, 111, 113
Tiles glazed, 113, 114
Topiary, 86, 161-167
Town gardens, 47, 116, 194-200
Trees linked with boundaries, 14, 63, 64-107
Trellis, 146, 167-171
Turf borders, 95
Turf paths, 96

V

Vases and Urns, 69, 104, 130, 177-183

W

Walls, 72-82, 105, 107, 151
Walls, retaining, 67, 124, 137, 150
Water, 6, 105, 106, 115, 172-177, 183, 185
West Wittering, Elm Tree Farm, 27, 35, 40, 44, 51, 84, 109, 116
Westerham, The Mount, 53, 55
Wild gardens, 17, 40

Y

Yew. *See* Hedges and Topiary

www.ingramcontent.com/pod-product-compliance
Lightning Source LLC
Chambersburg PA
CBHW070735160426
43192CB00009B/1453